THE ART OF MYSTERY

THE SEARCH FOR QUESTIONS

Also by Maud Casey

The Art of

MYSTERY

THE SEARCH FOR
QUESTIONS

Maud Casey

Graywolf Press

This publication is made possible, in part, by the voters of Minnesota through a Minnesota State Arts Board Operating Support grant, thanks to a legislative appropriation from the arts and cultural heritage fund, and through a grant from the Wells Fargo Foundation Minnesota. Significant support has also been provided by Target, the McKnight Foundation, the Lannan Foundation, the Amazon Literary Partnership, and other generous contributions from foundations, corporations, and individuals. To these organizations and individuals we offer our heartfelt thanks.

Published by Graywolf Press
250 Third Avenue North, Suite 600
Minneapolis, Minnesota 55401

www.graywolfpress.org

Published in the United States of America
Printed in Canada

ISBN 978-1-55597-794-8

2 4 6 8 9 7 5 3 1
First Graywolf Printing, 2018

Library of Congress Control Number: 2017937995

Cover design: Scott Sorenson

It is strange to be here. The mystery never leaves you alone.

—John O'Donohue

Contents

THE ART OF MYSTERY

THE SEARCH FOR QUESTIONS

The Land of Un

A few summers ago, I found myself pushing through hot, thick New York City air on Twenty-Third Street in Chelsea. I was on my way to be hypnotized. It was a pivotal point in my life—a long relationship was ending; life was supposed to have gone one way and it was about to go somewhere else entirely; there was about to be sadness, anger, guilt, the sensation of teetering on the edge of the earth with the possibility of, at any time, spinning off into the ether. The usual fare.

I was on my way to be hypnotized, and photographed in that hypnotic state. A friend of a friend, a photographer whose work I admired, was working on a project that involved photographing people for whom imagination plays a central role—artist, dancer, writer types. My friend had offered my name; at the time, I was working on a novel inspired by a nineteenth-century French psychiatric case study, which involved hypnosis, the medical intervention du jour, and the birth of photography as, among other things, a forensic tool for reading illness and criminality on the body. The photographer asked me to bring an important moment from my life, something to help focus me while being hypnotized. What felt most lacking in my life right then was wonder, and so I brought with me, like an ice cube in danger of melting in my hand before I arrived at the photographer's studio, my first memory of wonder.

In the very hot heat of the moment, jostling and being jostled by a sidewalk full of people with their own concerns, I felt that my concerns had shrunk themselves to this question: What if I'm one of those people who can't be hypnotized? When I arrived at the photographer's studio, while the photographer set up her tripod and the hypnotist explained the logistics in his deep and deeply soothing voice and I grew suspiciously drowsy, my concern suddenly flipped: What if I was so suggestible that I might be hypnotized before we even began? What ultimately happened lay somewhere in between resistance and submission; what happened was something that to this day I am unable to explain entirely.

I might begin, however, by telling you that my first memory of wonder is an impromptu camping trip in a Rhode Island pine forest, not far from the ocean, not far from where my family was living at the time. That it was possible my parents had been fighting (they were divorced not long after) and that, indeed, there was something fraught about my mother taking just us kids to the woods. That when we arrived in the woods, there was the sweet smell of pine and the sharp smell of ocean salt and in the distance the sound of crashing waves. That I was a painfully shy kid who spent much of her time willing invisibility around her like a cloak in the midst of a raucous bohemian family that occasionally lit itself on highly visible, glorious fire. That once night fell, it became so dark that the waves seemed to crash out of the darkness itself. What I felt then was part innocence, part terror, part awe. Something was revealed; something laid bare. It was to this wondrous place that I went under hypnosis.

I might also explain that I never completely lost the awareness of the photographer's studio, of the hypnotist, the photographer and her assistant. Even with my eyes closed, I could feel the hot flash of the bulb on the vintage tripod camera. I was, at once, performing and being magically transported to that place in the woods, a place, I would realize later, to which I'm transported on good days when I write. I might explain that I felt like myself and utterly unlike myself. I might try to explain all of these things, and I still wouldn't have gotten to the bottom of the experience. An experience I think about still, one I could think about endlessly. *What was that?*

We fiction writers talk a lot—for good reason, and to good end—about character, point of view, dialogue, scene, and summary, but in my experience, we don't talk a lot about mystery. It's not easy to talk about something that is a whispered invitation, a siren song, a flickering light in the distance. It's not easy to talk about something that, even as it encourages us to seek it, resists explanation. Something that wafts like smoke around the edges of the page. Especially when there is, in our culture, an increasing intolerance for ambiguity, for Keats's famous "negative capability," in which, as he wrote, one is "capable of being in uncertainties, Mysteries, doubts, without any irritable reaching after fact and reason."

But if stories are one of the ways we make sense of the world, they are also how we experience whatever doesn't make sense, whatever cannot be fully understood. Stories are how we stand in the presence of mystery. If mystery, the genre, is about finding the answers, then mystery, that elusive yet essential element of fiction, is about finding the questions. In Chekhov's famous letter to a friend, he wrote, "You are right to demand that an author take conscious stock of what he is doing, but you are confusing two concepts: *answering the questions* and *formulating them correctly*. Only the latter is required of an author." Mystery in fiction resides in those carefully articulated questions, and in the unparaphrasable content of a story or a novel, the experienced meaning.

I grew up in a home full of books—*Howards End*–style bookcases ready to kill us all, teetering stacks of books at the bottom of the stairs, a fan of books on the dining room table, piles of books on the back of toilets, books splayed open on the porch waiting patiently for someone to return. An embarrassment of riches—these portals to other worlds were everywhere. For a long time, subject to an eldest child's deference, I believed those other worlds belonged to my parents, whose books they were. They had, after all, walked through all of those portals long before me. But I was so wrong. Books are shape-shifting wild creatures no amount of reading can tame; so much depends on how we approach them, on what each of us, as readers, has to offer *them*. When I began to walk through those portals on my own, the endlessly expanding universe of mystery was there, waiting for me.

When one is, as one always is if one is paying any kind of attention, humbled by life, there's no getting out of this life without feeling an increasing sense of mystery. "Mystery isn't something that is gradually evaporating," Flannery O'Connor wrote in a letter. "It grows along with knowledge." This is true of the mystery we encounter in life, and it's true of the mystery we encounter in literature. I wouldn't have been able to articulate this quality at the beginning of my reading life, or the beginning of my writing life. Or even now. Not entirely. That's the thing about mystery: it remains just out of reach. Still, mystery has changed me and keeps changing me on a cellular level—among other things, it's made me a little less deferential, a little wilder. So here goes, my humble effort to sidle up to it.

Mystery in fiction has some things in common with the mystical experiences William James describes in the lectures he delivered in 1901 and 1902, which became *The Varieties of Religious Experience*. In them, he lays out four characteristics of the mystical experience: ineffability, a noetic quality, transiency, and what he describes as passivity (an initial effort must be made but then "the mystic feels as if his own will were in abeyance"), which is what readers do when they enter into a fictional world. In the end, James's project is not to minimize or dismiss conceptual processes or rational ones but to give value and credence to affective and visceral experience, which is what writers do when they fashion a fictional world out of words.

I find the most moving parts of James's *Varieties of Religious Experience* to be the personal testimony of people struggling to give voice to rare instances in which they were shaken free from the cage of self. Here are a few snippets: "But the more I seek words to express this intimate intercourse, the more I feel the impossibility of describing the thing by any of our usual images"; "As I sat there thinking, I seemed to feel some great and mighty presence"; "I only felt myself changed and believed myself another me; I looked for myself in myself and did not find myself." And my favorite: "I am undone." Slippery as religious experience, mystery involves an undoing that yields wonder.

Months later, when I returned to the photographer's studio to look at the proofs, I worried there would be no evidence of all those strange feelings. In the photographs, there I was, the fact of me, eyes closed. There was the fact of me, and then there was something else. Something enigmatic, suggestive of the innocence, terror, and awe, all those things I worried I'd only imagined. The photographer captured these layers. She captured the mystery of it all.

Under hypnosis, it's safe to say, I was undone. The photograph that resulted from the intersection of that experience and the photographer's eye undid me too.

Volunteering to be undone is not, perhaps, for everyone. But the question is—and it's a question every writer spends a lifetime thinking about—*What do we want art to be? What do we want it to do?* We don't, for example, usually ascribe the status of art to something that does one thing. To something that is, say, purely functional. Or that is only a morality tale. Or that only gets you off. Nor, I'm guessing, do we want art only to offer guidance or comfort. Art requires mystery. Mystery—often unclear, often involving unlikable characters, always involving unanswered questions, and often seriously weird and unsettling—requires plunging the reader into that Keatsian state of uncertainty and doubt. No irritable reaching after fact and reason. The reader should, in other words, be undone.

There's a lot that needs making in fiction but creating space for mystery requires a certain amount of unmaking. *Un*, that handy little prefix, is, as firefighters say about really big fires, fully involved. The good news is that *un* doesn't merely undo a word and turn it into its opposite; *un* is a release from, a freeing, a bringing out of, all of which are effects of mystery and part of its purpose. Mystery in fiction means taking the reader to that land of *Un*—uncertainty, unfathomability, unknowing. It's Kafka's axe to the frozen seas of our soul. In other words, it will—and it should—mess you up.

Admittedly, when we speak about mystery in fiction things can get a little, well, *mysterious*. "One can't write directly about the soul," Virginia Woolf wrote. "Looked at, it vanishes." I mean, how exactly does one paraphrase the unparaphrasable? How does one articulate experienced meaning, the kind that axes the frozen seas of our souls? Where is this ghostly electricity located, and how do you conjure it? It's a careful calibration, the cultivation of useful, inclusive mystery. It's the eternal authorial tightrope walk. How do we create inclusive, compelling mystery and avoid the kind that leaves a reader confounded to the point of throwing her out of the dream of the story? Eye of newt and toe of frog, wool of bat and tongue of dog? Yes, there's a bit of that, but there are other, less fanciful ways of coaxing mystery onto the page.

What follows is an investigation into some of those ways: the construction of innocence; character—two varieties in particular, those who keep secrets and those who are contradictory and/or absurd; imagery; embedding mystery in structure; through ghosts and other spectral presences. This book will include close readings of high-wire acts by a number of authors, some of whom are well known and some less well known, whose fiction undoes me. My consideration of this rich subject is by no means comprehensive. Mystery in literature, as in life, expresses itself in infinite ways.

Unknowing,
or The Construction of Innocence

In 1873, the spirit photographer Édouard Buguet made a name for himself among the Spiritualist crowd. He did this by taking photographs of, among others, the Spiritualist Lady Caithness and her son Count de Medina Pomar, to whom thirteen distinct spirits appeared, including Lady Caithness's late husband, who brought with him from the other world an apple, part of the family crest, as proof of his identity and his realness. In 1875, police raided Buguet's studio on the boulevard Montmartre in Paris. They confiscated two dummies, shrouds, fake beards, and hundreds of pictures of life-sized heads glued onto cards. At his trial, Buguet caved completely and confessed to double-exposing his plates with these props. As he explained to the court, he would construct an approximation of the dead person with whom his client wished to be photographed and then, while his receptionist chatted up the client, he would photograph the dummy dead person set against a dark background and obscured by a "fluidic veil" to disguise the rough edges. He showed the court how he used the same portrait to serve as this person's dead mother and that person's dead sister and this other person's dead friend. The prosecution brought in as many former Buguet clients as they could find as witnesses against him, including a journalist, a professor of history, a colonel of artillery, an optician, and, most notably, a photographic expert. Each of them listened to Buguet explain the deception, and every one of them, in the face of Buguet's confession of guilt, testified in his defense.

This is a story of many things. Gullibility, sure. Pride, coupled with a bit of the customer is always right, or the customer always *wants* to be right. No one wants to be a sucker, and these people had paid good money for a picture of themselves with their dead beloveds. But there is something else going on here too: often we humans, out of love, out of loss, sometimes for no reason at all, want to believe. As a story about the desire for story itself, I find it not only moving but also quite resonant for us human writers.

Modern Spiritualism, as it happens, began a few years after Morse invented the telegraph, a system in which messages were transmitted, as if by ghostly magic, over great distances. It was a time when new technology—X-rays, for example—allowed people to see invisible things. The very structure of Spiritualism, which believed in the materialization of the dead, was deeply aligned with, constructed out of, the technology and science of the era. It was, in its way, the poetry of that era's technology and science.

We don't turn to fiction for the facts. Fiction offers relief from the facts and from that terrible word—*closure.* In her essay "You Need Not Doubt What I Say Because It Is Not True," Marilynne Robinson describes the way, in regular life, we are usually vigilant about the existence of reality. After all, it's what divides the sane from the insane. But, she writes, "Fiction relieves us of this defensiveness—in fiction we expect surprise, irony, reversal. In effect, we expect to be fooled." And, sometimes, like the people who wanted nothing more than to believe the trickster spirit photographer, we yearn to be fooled.

Spirit photography offers an apt analogy for the seductive quality of literary mystery; each is highly crafted and succeeds only if a certain amount of mystery is conjured and maintained. One of the ways this happens in fiction is by the author's creating a sophisticated structure that evokes, even encourages, innocence. (That *is* the ghost of my beloved!)

Writing within the same relentlessly guilty historical moment in Eastern Europe in the 1920s, Isaac Babel and Dezső Kosztolányi each construct a variety of defiant innocence. Babel, in his short story "Awakening," from his self-proclaimed *Autobiographical Stories* (1923–25), and Kosztolányi, in his novel *Skylark* (1924), invite readers into possibility spaces to engage with things that cannot be grasped by reason. Fiction, after all, is a democratic art, reliant on the participation of its citizen readers, and in the best circumstances, readers are contemporaneously sent back into themselves and out into the larger universe.

This is certainly what happened to me when as a kid I picked up Babel's *Autobiographical Stories* off the top of a teetering stack of books in my parents' house and walked through its portal. What I encountered in these stories was the mystery one must evoke to become a writer. Uncertainty is not just a by-product of the vocation, these stories suggest; it should be courted. Babel's *ars poetica* is based not on the logic of what we can know, but on the logic, if you will, of uncertainty, of what we can feel. Babel himself was a mystery. In the introduction to the 1955 edition of Isaac Babel's *Collected Stories*, the first edition published in English, long after his murder by Stalin, Lionel Trilling described Babel's approach to fiction: The reader "ought not be given what he can easily recognize as 'a certified true copy' of life" because "the human fact does not dominate the scene of our existence—for something to 'show forth' it must first be hidden, and the human fact is submerged in and subordinated to a world of circumstance." Babel was his own hidden human fact. So much about Babel was a puzzle, a question. Part of this was political—he was a writer living in the midst of a fascist regime, serving, and being censored, at the pleasure of Stalin, protected only because of his connection to the writer Maksim Gorky. There was the mystery of his death, only resolved in the 1990s when it was possible to gain access to the KGB archives that said, yes, Stalin had Babel executed soon after his arrest in 1939. Perhaps Babel's own cuspy state lent itself to the production of mystery in his writing.

The Odessa of Babel's story "Awakening" is based on the Odessa of Babel's childhood, a place where coming of age traditionally meant taking up the mantle of musical genius expected of every Jewish kid. Mr. Zagursky is the violin teacher (based on Babel's own famous violin teacher) who has been sending these wunderkinds into the world as virtuosos for decades. The story is a narrator looking back on his thirteen-year-old-boy self, who would rather be reading Turgenev and Dumas than practicing violin; who starts cutting class and heading to the Odessa port, far from his home and his violin lessons, where glamorously knowing, macho teenage boys loiter. The narrator yearns to slip the traces of the scholarly traditions of his community so he might fit in, but stronger still is his desire to make these cool boys who "dived under the barges, stole coconuts for dinner and awaited the time when the steamerfuls of water-melon would drift slowly in from Kherson and Kamenka, and those water-melons could be split open on the moorings of the port" vivid to an audience. To this observant, writerly kid, they are potential material!

An older man, a proofreader who lives by the port, takes it upon himself to teach the boys to swim. He takes a particular interest in the narrator, who is a really terrible swimmer. When the proofreader/mentor reads something the narrator has written he recognizes "a spark of the divine." But, he cautions the boy, in order to become a writer, you must know the name of every-thing in nature—the names of birds and trees, for example. The narrator is left baffled by this. He has grown up in a scholarly, textcentric culture; nature was not a big part of the conversation. How is he meant to become a writer if a language he has not yet learned constricts him?

At the end of the story, the narrator dreams of "escape"—not only from Odessa but also into the world of his imagination, where he might chisel stories out of sentences: "The moonlight froze on unknown bushes, on trees that had no name. An invisible bird gave a peep and was silent—perhaps it had fallen asleep. What kind of bird was it? What was its name? Is there dew in the evening? Where is the constellation of Great Bear situated? In what direction does the sun rise?" The narrator wants to know these things, but the beauty of the moment has to do with *not* knowing. It is decentering, disorienting, and yet knowing less becomes a means to a different kind of knowing more.

Let me offer a kindred model from a champion cinematic digressor. For his 2010 documentary *Cave of Forgotten Dreams* Werner Herzog was granted exclusive access by the French government to the Cave of Chauvet-Pont-d'Arc in southern France, containing thirty-two-thousand-year-old cave paintings. As his camera pans over the rough-hewn horses, reindeer,

rhinos, and bison, these animals appear to be gallop-
ing, thanks in part to their creators' ingenious use of
the undulations of the cave walls to create the illusion
of movement, as well as to Herzog's ingenious use of
3-D. That there are layers of these creatures, painted
by Paleolithic nomads over the course of some two
thousand years, makes them all the more breathtaking.
You are looking at art; you are looking at time; you are
looking at something difficult to apprehend from your
fixed position in the twenty-first century. With his
trademark goofy gusto, Herzog interviews lab-coated
scientists in a room filled with computers that provide
stratigraphic analyses and laser scans to map every inch
of the cave. He is fascinated by the scientists' scrutiny
of the layers of paint that has allowed them to deter-
mine which of the paintings were done by the cave artist missing one finger (he was prolific) and which of the
paintings were done thousands of years later. But he's
just as interested in hearing about the dreams of one of
these scientists, in which he wakes up inside the cave
with the bones of saber-toothed tigers. He's also interested in this particular scientist's former career as a
unicyclist (and encourages, one might even say incites,
digressions in his interviews). Scientific facts? Yes, up
to a point, but Herzog's not an expert and that non-
expert vantage point is the one from which he wants his
audience to regard these cave paintings. He wants you

to wander off with him to consult the former president of the French Society of Perfumers, who roves around mountainsides, sniffing for cave vapors—this passionate sniffing is part of the experience of the cave paintings, too. His stance stubbornly resists infiltration by expertise; he protects the cave from an avalanche of scientific data. By doing this, he opens up a space at the center of the cave and that space is where a generative mystery may flourish. "What constitutes humanness?" he asks a group of archeologists. As Herzog's camera waltzes you around the cave (to eye-rollingly melodramatic music but, whatever, it's all part of the Herzogian experience), you follow his lead and you find yourself thinking, What *does* constitute humanness? Who were those cave painters? Who am I? What is the soul? What is art? Herzog dances you into this state of awe; dances you into a state of innocence.

Babel creates a similar dance (to very different music) in that penultimate moment's swirl of questions in "Awakening." Sometimes mystery in a narrative depends on creating a space in the center of the story's cave, a space that is protected from an avalanche of data. In 1934, Babel was invited to speak, as a Stalin-approved writer, at the Soviet-sponsored Writers' Congress. The speech he gave, five years before his arrest, was laced with double entendre, coded and heartbreaking. He described himself as "the master of the genre of silence."

He was referring to the impossibility of writing in a totalitarian society that forbade independent thinking, but might he also have been referring to a silence that leaves room for mystery, cultivated in his work long before he had to be so careful? In "Awakening," there is a silence at the end of the story where in the hands of another writer there might have been a flood of words. The narrator might have spoken from a place of knowledge, answering all of the questions he poses, naming everything: the Siberian pine; the great crested grebe; yes, there is dew in the evening; the Great Bear constellation is situated *there*; the sun rises in the east. This, by the way, would not have improved the passage.

Writing at the same time as Babel, Virginia Woolf, in her 1924 essay "Mr. Bennett and Mrs. Brown," describes the benefits of emphasizing something other than "the fabric of things." In her meditation on how best to describe the character of Mrs. Brown, the old woman in the train car, she imagines the advice of those she calls the "great Edwardians": "'Begin by saying that her father kept a shop in Harrogate. Ascertain the rent. Ascertain the wages of shop assistants in the year 1878. Discover what her mother died of. Describe cancer. Describe calico. Describe—' But I cried: 'Stop! Stop!'" Woolf is being cheeky, but she ends by saying that all of this stuff, all of this information, would have caused *her* Mrs. Brown, "that vision to which I cling though I know no way of imparting it to you," to disappear. To be clear, she and Babel are not anti-knowledge. At the end of Babel's story, the value of all those names is never in question. But names are not the point. The point is to achieve the impossible—to move beyond language toward an evanescent, evasive experience unmediated by names.

Dezső Kosztolányi's novel *Skylark* has a lovely and deceptive simplicity. Even before the events of the novel begin to unfold, Kosztolányi has sealed it in a shimmering soap bubble of historical innocence. Kosztolányi, who was born in 1885 and died in 1936, happily enjoying some literary celebrity during his relatively short lifetime, began writing *Skylark* in 1923. It was published in 1924. But the events of *Skylark* take place in the retrospectively portentous year of 1899. It relies on the delicate bubble of the fictional Sárszeg (Kosztolányi's hometown), floating in blissful, political ignorance of the giant pin of history waiting on the other side of the new century. A lot happened between 1899 and 1924, the year *Skylark* was published—among other things, the demise of the Austro-Hungarian Empire, World War I, a number of Hungarian revolutions. The fictional world of *Skylark* doesn't understand that the rest of the world is about to fall. It is an artificial construction Kosztolányi is well aware of, and he wants us to be aware of it too, evident in fleeting instances of outside perspectives—"haughty Budapesters" who deign to peek out of the windows of trains passing through.

This exquisite innocence creates a fairy-tale effect, beginning with the subtitle of chapter one, "in which the reader is introduced to an elderly couple and their daughter, the apple of their eye, and hears of complicated preparations for a trip to the plains." It is a simple premise with a neat, uncomplicated structure: a woman named Skylark, the aforementioned apple, who has never left home, never been away from her elderly parents, goes away to spend a week with cousins on the Hungarian plains. Her parents, the Vajkays, referred to mostly as Mother and Father, are left alone for the first time. Their world—Sárszeg—which until now has been all "silence and solitude," becomes as glorious a discovery as a cave painting filmed in 3-D.

But first, a bit more about that apple, Skylark. Here's the rub: the apple of Mother and Father's eye is not beautiful. In fact, she is ugly. Not ugly as in duckling, not ugly as in beautiful on the inside, not ugly as in possessing a heightened sense of morality or deeper wisdom than the rest of the world. She is ugly ugly. Obviously, *ugly* is as subjective a term as *beautiful*, and Kosztolányi knows this.

In his book *The Fairytale as Art Form and Portrait of Man*, the Swiss scholar of fairy tales Max Lüthi describes a phenomenon called "the shock effect of beauty." The idea is that, in fairy tales, beauty is abstract, its actual form never specified; the lack of specification is part of its power. "Beauty is more perfect in the representation engendered by the word than in the actual world." The word *beauty* creates a vista for the imagination. Beauty is meant to be mysterious and its effect puzzling. In fairy tales, after all, beauty causes people to faint dead away and, on occasion, to drop dead. Its absence of definition is part of its mystery-generating power.

Skylark's ugliness is without qualification and it is rendered with the same lack of specificity as the beauty described by Lüthi's beauty shock. We are told Skylark waddles like a duck, that her face is pudgy, her eyes watery, but these are broad strokes in the same way Sleeping Beauty's porcelain skin and ruby red lips are broad strokes. *Ugly* is the bald word Kosztolányi uses, and he means for it to be shocking. It's what her parents secretly think of her but would never say out loud: she is an ugly old maid whose stifling presence all these years has kept them under a kind of spell. The word *ugly* and the space around it cast a spell on the reader as well.

Until Skylark leaves, we are told Father has spent his days looking backward, studying genealogies; he prefers his ancestors to his own future, which holds not much except his own death. Until Skylark leaves, Mother and Father have always woken promptly at seven, which is when Skylark begins cleaning. Until she leaves, they use only one of four lightbulbs in the living room chandelier to save money on electricity. Until she leaves, they eat only the bland food she cooks for them, never eating out. There are no sensual pleasures when Skylark's around, and there are no pleasures of the imagination either. In the days before Skylark left, there was no room for the imagination. Father was so occupied with "stimulating, edifying books which elucidated some moral truth" that he "wouldn't even look at a work on which imagination had left its magic mark." Skylark, we are told, could never go to the theater because the crowds overwhelmed her and she had anxiety attacks. But once she's gone, the spell lifts. For the first time since they can remember, the couple oversleeps! They screw in those other three lightbulbs! Mother plays the piano that has remained untouched for years! Though the couple remains uninterested in not-yet-historical events looming on the political horizon (the Dreyfus affair, yawn), the newspaper has a sudden, unfamiliar appeal! "Foreign news items flashed up before them, charging the air they breathed with a buzz of electricity, connecting the couple to the burning, bitter, but not entirely ignominious, or worthless, affairs of the outside world. They didn't understand much of what they read, but felt none the less that they were not entirely alone." And they aren't as alone as they were. When Skylark leaves, they eat out every night at the King of Hungary, the local restaurant, where they not only contemplate eating vanilla noodles ("What exactly can they be? I've never tried them, never even seen them," thinks Father), they *eat* vanilla noodles! They dine with the A-list of Sárszeg—the commander in chief of the fire brigade and actors with whom Father smokes a cigar! This week without Skylark is a week of downright bedazzlement.

The pinnacle is their trip to the theater to see *The Geisha*, a musical comedy set in a country almost as foreign to the Vajkays as its subject—romantic love. Here, in this parallel universe, in this fairy-tale town teetering on the brink of the war-torn twentieth century, the couple is led to the well of imagination, where they eagerly drink. They are made drunk, it is that mystifying. Neither Father nor Mother recognizes the actors they've dined with at the King of Hungary, so transformed, so transported, are they. Father is filled with "unfamiliar sensations," so "utterly bewitched" he shocks himself by stuttering with praise and awe in front of the leading lady at the end of the play. It serves as a metacommentary on the importance of mystery in art. The Vajkays have been seduced into the innocence that art conjures, and we along with them. Father and Mother, and we along with them, are willing to be duped for the sake of transcending ordinary experience in the name of astonishment. We want to give ourselves over to the unfamiliar. We want to be bewitched. We want to be undone.

But the extraordinary relies on the ordinary for its existence. It cannot last forever; if it did, it wouldn't be extraordinary. The week must end and Skylark must return in the same way 1899 will eventually click over into the new century. Still, as a result of the startling experiences they've had in the world that's been there all along, a fierce light is shone on the thing that has remained in the shadows. Father says the word that neither he nor his wife has ever, ever uttered: *ugly*. Skylark is ugly. Mother does the only thing she can do: she denies it. She sews the rent fabric of their lives back up, sewing even as she does not believe her own argument, even as her sewing reveals the haphazard seams. And when Skylark returns and asks what happened while she was gone, her mother says, "We were waiting for you, that's all."

Once you have beheld the cave paintings, you are altered. What you see cannot be unseen. What is undone cannot ever, truly, be done back up again—the stitches of that haphazard seam show. This couple will never be the same again. What has been made possible by clearing a space for mystery is transformative. It changes us, forever. Kosztolányi performs a narrative

sleight of hand at the end of his novel that at once reveals this and breaks our hearts. Once Skylark is safely
ensconced at home again, once Father has declared the
food at the King of Hungary restaurant wretched and
Skylark has promised to cook something very bland
to restore everyone to good health, there is an unexpected shift into Skylark's perspective:

> But during her week away, far from her parents,
> something had changed inside her, something she
> only became aware of now. . . .
>   'I,' she began in her thoughts, as we all do when
> thinking of ourselves.
>   But this I was her, something, someone whose life
> she really lived. She was this I, in body and in soul,
> one with its very flesh, its memories, its past, present
> and future, all of which we seal into a single destiny
> each time we face ourselves and utter that tiny, un-
> alterable word: 'I.'

Now it is Skylark's turn to marvel. With this,
Kosztolányi throws open a window in the house of his
novel and the view we have is of ourselves. Who am I?
What is the soul? What constitutes humanness?

At the end of the novel, Skylark sobs into her pil-
low so her parents in the adjacent room won't hear her;
meanwhile on the other side of the wall, Father and

Mother chatter in an attempt to fill the silence of the abyss. "Our little bird has finally flown home," Father says. Kosztolányi leaves us in the hollow inside the wall that separates these characters, an echo chamber of feeling in which the poignancy of the foolhardy bravery required to answer Forster's call to *only connect* resounds, and we are left to contemplate the mystery of the human condition. In "Awakening," Babel's narrator is made to understand all he doesn't know; Kosztolányi's characters are made to unknow all they think they understand.

And then there are the times we *know*, but we continue to beat our heads against the wall of the answer in the hopes of cracking it open to reveal something else. A willful evasion that allows for mystery. This is a subject Amy Hempel's fiction often features. In her sly short story "What Were the White Things?" about a woman avoiding a doctor's appointment that will likely deliver bad news, the question of the title becomes a refrain. The narrator asks it first in reference to the objects in the paintings at an exhibit the narrator has ducked into impulsively (the exhibit is called, notably, "Finding the Mystery in Clarity"); she asks it again in reference to the things she chose to take when her enraged mother was, ominously, giving away all of her possessions; she asks it when she finally does get

�᷅ see below

herself to the doctor and he shows her an X-ray that is definitely not good news. And when the doctor explains precisely what the white things are on the slide, the narrator asks the question yet again. Here is the last paragraph of the story: "The doctor said he would explain it to me again, and proceeded to tell me a second time. He asked me if this time I understood what he had told me. Yes, I said. I said, Yes, but what were the white things?"

The beginning of cinema occurred contemporaneously with the golden age of spirit photography. There were several early films—G. A. Smith's *Photographing a Ghost* (1898), Georges Méliès's *The Spiritualist Photographer* (1903)—whose very subject was the techniques the spirit photographers were using to manipulate their photographs in their studios. In other words, their fraudulent nature was no big secret even in their heyday. For the people who wanted to be reunited with their beloveds, the truth was not what they were after. *Yes*, those people who wanted to be undone said. *Yes*, but what were the white things?

Mystery in Character:
A Secret Life with a Secret

The privacy of the singular mind, the privacy of consciousness, is one of fiction's exceptional gifts to us. Character is fiction's mechanism for delivering this exceptional gift. *Mechanism* is perhaps too mechanical a word for character, that invaluable element of fiction to which E. M. Forster devoted not one but two chapters in his seminal book about fiction, *Aspects of the Novel*. He titled these chapters "People" and "People (*Continued*)." Characters, these wholly invented creatures, feel that real. Character, that warp and weft of an inimitable consciousness, is at the very heart of literature, and so, following Forster's lead, I've devoted two chapters to it.

I recently saw a documentary about the photographer Vivian Maier, whose magnificently odd and intimate photographs were discovered only after her death. The self-portraits where she isn't even there are the ones I like best. In one, she is a shadow on a lawn, a shimmer in the shiny head of a sprinkler. A shadow sliver of her wide-brimmed hat and her broad shoulders on the sidewalk at the feet of two women, creamy legs crossed on a bench, leaning into conversation. A shadow puppet, dancing on the side of a Chicago building. She is several shadows at the beach. In one, trees grow out of her shadow head; in another, possibly my favorite, the shadow brim of her hat almost touches the hair-rollered head of a sunbathing woman.

I keep misremembering the title of the film. There's a reason for this stubborn amnesia relevant to thinking about mystery and character. *I wanted to figure out who she was*, says John Maloof in this film he cowrote and codirected with Charlie Siskel. Maloof's the intrepid, endearing guy who discovered the treasure trove of Maier's photographs—more than a hundred thousand negatives!—at a thrift auction house in Chicago and made them public after her death. *Why is a nanny taking all these photos?* Maloof asks. The only unimaginative part of the film involves the unimaginative questions—*Why is she childless? Why is she unmarried?*—discernible in the subtext of interviews conducted with her employers and the children in her care. There was also her stubborn eccentricity. *Why does she speak with a possibly fake French accent?* The woman with the twin-lens Rolleiflex camera was a mystery.

Here's the misremembering part. I keep insisting the documentary is called *In Search of Vivian Maier*. What it's really called is *Finding Vivian Maier*. Why is this relevant? Because Maier was a mystery fascinated by the mystery of the self. She understood there's only ever *in search of*, never *finding*. No pinning the butterfly—its roving expansive wanderings, the poignant flapping against its cage. Maier took lots of photographs—intimate, wonderfully strange street photographs as good as, sometimes better than, Garry Winogrand's and Diane Arbus's. But it is the self-portraits in stark black and white, the color of the world bled out, their smoky elusivity, that I can't stop looking at. They contain questions. Am I her? *Her?* Am I *here*? She is a secret even to herself.

Forster famously described the "secret lives" of characters as the essential part of creating a singular character. The most potent characters, like the Maier portraits, make us feel as though we're standing in the presence of a very particular someone, in the presence of a very particular sensibility. There is the suggestion of the greater mystery of the self—in motion, fluid, never static—which exceeds the page. Forster writes of characters, "And this is why they often seem more definite than characters in history, or even our own friends; we have been told all about them that can be told; even if they are imperfect or unreal they do not contain any secrets, whereas our friends do and must, mutual secrecy being one of the conditions of life upon this globe." But sometimes making room for the mystery of the self means allowing a character to have secrets the way our friends do and must. It means creating a secret life with a secret.

The protagonists of Barbara Comyns's novel *The Vet's Daughter* and Paul Yoon's novel *Snow Hunters* have secret lives to which the reader has access and secrets to which the reader does not. In other words, you are aware they are keeping things from you, these characters. Though Alice Rowland and Yohan are quite different—Alice is the seventeen-year-old daughter of an abusive English veterinarian in suburban London in the 1950s; Yohan is a North Korean refugee who, in 1954, accepts an offer from the UN to emigrate to a Brazilian port town—each of these authors has a deep, abiding interest in the texture of a particularly nimble mind navigating an ill-lit corner of the world. What is on the page is one piece torn from a whole cloth. In other words, there is more. In each instance, this creates useful mystery. Rather than obscuring the characters, their secrets add to their allure.

Barbara Comyns, who is not as well known as she should be, may require a bit of an introduction. She wrote eleven novels with spectacular titles between 1947 and 1989—*Who Was Changed and Who Was Dead* and *Our Spoons Came from Woolworths* among them—before her death in 1992. One of the more recent efforts to rescue her from the dustbin of history is the beautiful edition of *The Vet's Daughter*, originally published in 1959, put out by the *New York Review of Books* with a foreword by Kathryn Davis. On the cover is a reproduction of a painting by Louise Bourgeois that at first you might mistake for lovely red stockings hanging on a clothesline but, look closer: those aren't lovely red stockings, that's bloody sinew and bone. The painting's title is *Untitled (Legs and Bones)*.

The double-take experience of the cover (Lovely red stockings! Oh, wait, body parts . . .) is an apt introduction to the novel itself, which is simultaneously beautiful and terrifying. If this subtly layered story is a kind of fairy tale, then Alice Rowland is its Cinderella destined to remain in the ashes. Her father, the veterinarian of the title, is a sinister, outsized villain who sports—for real!—a waxed-tip mustache. His closest friend is a vivisectionist and, in the name of efficiency, he has his sick wife measured for her coffin while she's still alive. The sad-then-dead mother is, but of course, replaced by an evil stepmother who tries to pawn Alice off on a pervy friend of hers. It's grim. But wait! One night, about fifty pages into this tale of woe, while lying in bed after yet another dreary day of tending to the lame mongoose and polishing the monkey skull her father keeps for display, Alice levitates. She is as astonished as we are. She is also so isolated, so out of touch, that she has no idea if floating above one's bed in the middle of the night is normal or not. "Perhaps," she wonders poignantly, "it was something that often happened to people but was never mentioned, like piles." Her secret levitations continue until her villainous father, discovering her at it, sees a chance to make a buck off his freaky daughter and takes it.

In *The Vet's Daughter*, you are made aware from the very first line that Alice is keeping things from you, that there is a secret life to this secret life. The first line is this: "A man with small eyes and a ginger moustache came and spoke to me when I was thinking of something else." Comyns introduces us to Alice as she is having a private thought, and we will never learn what that private thought, that *something else*, is. And so Comyns conveys, somewhat radically to my mind, the sense of a character who, even in the deep-space privacy of a first-person narrative, has secrets from the reader. This exists, Alice's most private self, Comyns is saying, and I want you to consider it, too. I want you to consider it first. This is especially important because Alice's odd and oddly compelling sensibility is the engine of the novel. In other words, mousy, pathetic, exploited Alice is bigger than the life to which she is shackled. Listen to her voice:

> The sun came slanting in through the window and touched the mantelpiece, where the monkey's skull used to lie. I placed a damp log on the recently lighted fire. A soft hissing sound came and a frantic woodlouse rushed about the smoking bark. I rescued it with a teaspoon, although I had no fondness for woodlice. It was a pity to let it burn—and there it was, squirming on the damp teaspoon, grey and

rather horrible. With one hand I pushed up the window and with the other placed it on the sill, where it
crawled about leaving a small wet trail of tea among
the winged sycamore-seeds that had lodged there.
The air was sharp and wintry, and the street very still.
The only people to be seen were a few pale women
with black string bags. Under the gate a dried leaf
rustled very gently. I thought, 'It's minutes like this
that seem to last so long.'

The sensibility at work here is akin to a strange
forensic detective—a member of the CSI team gone a
bit off. That keen, idiosyncratic eye takes in every stark
little detail—that slanting bit of sun on the mantel
where the weird monkey's skull used to lie. And then,
simultaneously, along with that almost clinical observation, there is an eerie, expectant innocence. The *still
street*, as if something is about to happen. The *few pale
women with black string bags*, fairy-tale figures in an
apocalyptic world that is also waiting, poised. What's
in those bags? Who are these women? This painfully
observant mind, naive but curious, presses itself against
the brutal world waiting for the secret panel to give
way onto a hidden stash of beauty. That detective's
eye notices even the hidden place under the gate. It
animates the dead leaf it finds there—it may be dead,
but it's still in motion. *Rustled* (the verb indicates con-

tinuity and so, in its teeny way, is hopeful) *very gently* (there is a tenderness in her attitude toward the things of this world). The passage is metonymic, suggesting not only what Alice is noticing but also the way she notices. She is hyperobservant by virtue of being an outsider to everything she sees.

There's a lot of talk about the way fiction unites us, bridges difference, connects us. But it seems useful too to consider the ways fiction divides us. As in: wow, look at that, here is this mind moving through this minute in a manner wholly unfamiliar to me. How weird her syntactical navigations. How pleasingly eccentric her diction. How mysterious. There is more to Alice and her energetic mind than we will ever know, Comyns announces with the opening line; Alice's consciousness is infinite, spilling over the boundaries of a novel.

Isak Dinesen wrote, "There is no mystery in art. Do the things you can see, they will show you what you cannot see." In other words, there *is* mystery in art, but one of the ways it is conjured occurs when an author lavishes narrative attention on the visible. With Comyns, the visible is sometimes the minutiae—the "frantic woodlouse" and the "winged sycamore-seeds." These phrases alert the reader to the possibility, the likelihood, of miraculous detail everywhere else.

Doing the things you can see means attending to the tactile details. In Alice's earnest description of her levitations, it's precisely the gritty ordinariness of the details she chooses to observe that makes the scenes so extraordinary. Here is an excerpt from the first time Alice levitates:

> When I returned home Rosa [the evil stepmother] and Father were drinking port in the dining-room, and the beef that was boiling in the kitchen was nearly dry and the carrots had stuck to the bottom of the saucepan. I added more water, and balls of dough to make dumplings. The dumplings swelled up huge and danced in the boiling gravy, and the kitchen was filled with steam. Water poured down the windows like rain inside out. I began to think I could hear water pouring and falling. Then I thought I could see it, and it was as if floods had come, and everywhere there was water very grey and silvery, and I seemed to be floating above it. I came to a mountain made of very dark water; but, when I reached the top, it was a water garden where everything sparkled. Although the water was rushing very fast, it always stayed in the same beautiful shapes, and there were fountains and trees and flowers all shimmering as if made of moving ice.

Alice doesn't know the word for what is happening to her (she doesn't find out until much later in the book).

Because the experience isn't reduced to its name, she is further alienated from the already alienating experience. There is an amplification of the strange; the reader hears it in stereo. Comyns's commitment to the mundane details and to Alice's physical, sensory experience cultivates the sort of mystery that invites us to enter into it. Here is where we can contemplate the big questions, among them, *How do we hold emotion in our bodies and what happens when emotion is uncontainable?* As Alice Munro writes in her story "Epilogue: The Photographer" from *Lives of Girls and Women*, "People's lives, in Jubilee as elsewhere, were dull, simple, amazing and unfathomable—deep caves paved with kitchen linoleum."

When the BBC approached Comyns about making a serial version of *The Vet's Daughter* for radio, they told her they planned to make the levitations happen in a dream. But you can't do that, Comyns objected, they're real. It's their realness—the shimmering visions coupled always with concrete details (the steam-filled kitchen, the boiling gravy)—that makes them so unsettling. Alice doesn't talk much about her father's cruelty, never explicitly. In the anxiety over breaking the lamp globe is the anxiety of a daughter whose father shows her no love at all. In these levitation scenes, Comyns suggests what Alice is unable to tell the reader, or even herself, directly. Comyns's insistence on the

realness of them has to do with her belief that the solid-
ity of the real casts a shadow that will contain everything
else, all that's not spelled out yet is deeply felt—the rest
of Alice, her potential self, the part of her so fierce she
rises up.

In his deceptively spare, elegant novel *Snow Hunters*,
Paul Yoon fashions a different secret-life-with-a-secret,
allowing us to experience an unlikely, paradoxical intimacy with a laconic character haunted by the trauma
of war. As with Comyns, one sentence does a lot of work
in generating a force field of mystery.

The present action of the novel is simple. Twenty-
five-year-old Yohan has accepted an offer from the UN
to emigrate to a port town in Brazil rather than repa-
triate to North Korea after two years in an American
prison camp during the Korean War. He doesn't speak
the language in his adopted country (which accounts
for some of his quietness, but not all of it). He has no
family, no home, and he has come to a place where
he is surrounded by "lives that all seemed unknowable and closed as though oceans surrounded each of
them." Yohan's life, too, appears at first to the reader as
unknowable and closed to the people who surround
him. This is deliberate on Yoon's part. You find yourself leaning into the silence that surrounds Yohan as
he finds work as an assistant to a Japanese tailor, as he

slowly learns Portuguese, as he makes tentative friend-
ships with other people as dislocated as he is, including two orphaned children. His relationships have an
intimacy that has little to do with words. The novel is
very interested in the possibilities of silence as a space
for tenderness and connection that go well beyond language; it asks us to pay close attention to this man who
might otherwise pass invisibly through the landscape.
Then, in short bursts and at increasing volume over the
course of the novel, we begin to get snatches of memories from Yohan's two years in the prison camp—the
way he vomited daily when he was forced to move the
dead out of the camp and salvage their clothes, until
he no longer felt enough to vomit; how he watched
a river catch fire; the way he found an anonymous
foot sticking out of the ground. These impressionistic
glimpses accumulate. They contribute to, and begin to
account for, the exquisite surface tension of the novel
in the present. Yohan is a ghost, and he is haunted.

The mystery-generating sentence occurs early in the
novel, in the midst of Yohan's first memory of the war.
As with all of the memories to come, Yoon launches
us into the past with something we can see, a physical
object that becomes the associative link between past
and present: in this case, the gray suit Yohan is wearing
when he gets off the boat in Brazil. It's too big for him,
we are told, and then we learn it's the suit he was given

to wear on the day he left the camp. A young American nurse took the military shirt he wore for two years and gently, meticulously folded it though it was near rags. Her kindness was one of the only kindnesses Yohan experienced during those years "but he did not tell her so" because this is a novel that pays attention to all that is said and to everything that goes unsaid, those unspoken words floating all around us. Yohan puts on the too-big suit and gets in the UN truck that will take him away from his home forever. And here's the sentence: "From a tower someone waved. He shut his eyes and thought of castles."

What castles? He doesn't tell us, and he will never tell us. After I finished *Snow Hunters*, I wrote Yoon because that line haunted me. He wrote back and said, funny, that was a line that many people suggested he cut. When I asked how he justified keeping the line, this is what he wrote:

> I wanted Yohan to have privacy. I wanted him to have secrets no one else can access. This felt true to me. In life we're surrounded by friends and family who carry their own secrets and I thought it should work the same in fiction. There are parts of Yohan no one can access, whether that be another character or even the reader. We get to that line and we ask ourselves: what castles? And in raising that question my hope was

that rather than feel like we don't know Yohan, we know him more deeply, having caught a glimpse into something so very private.

Many years ago, I worked as a secretary at the Lee Strasberg Theatre Institute in New York City, which included cleaning up after an incontinent dog named Colette and sorting through the detritus of Marilyn Monroe's estate—shoes, pillboxes, garlic presses (this was before it was all put on the auction block). Part of my job was archiving videotapes of Lee Strasberg teaching acting classes. I only ever made it through half of the 1970s—there was a lot of suede fringe and feathered hair. One of the Stanislavsky-inspired exercises Strasberg taught his students was called the "private moment." The private moment involves performing something you would normally do when no one else was around: looking in the mirror; picking your toenails; one guy really went for it and simulated masturbation (I felt bad for him). The idea is to be as natural as possible, to not perform at all, to give the audience a glimpse into something private, the sort of thing we do when no one else is around, something we only see the surface of because what we're watching is someone turned inward.

The secret of the secret life in fiction might be considered a technique analogous to the private moment in Method acting. We watch Yohan have a private moment, in which we see the surface of a thought, but because of the vividness of Yohan's overlarge gray coat, and because we have been told about the kind nurse, the gesture toward everything that we don't know about Yohan doesn't frustrate; rather, it intrigues. The thought about the castle that goes unexplained is one car of a larger train of thought. It is evidence of a bounteous, textured mind. With it, the math of Yohan suddenly gets even more complex.

You may be thinking I'm making too much of these sentences in novels that have pages and pages and pages of sentences. But these fleeting moments—there it went—are critical parts of a literary aesthetic that favors gesture over explanation. A runway is carefully constructed out of concrete detail from which the narrative can lift off into a more ethereal, private realm.

There's another such gesture worth pointing out in *Snow Hunters* that allows for this liftoff to happen. Yohan finds himself in the shanty settlement on the edge of town where his friends, the orphaned children, are staying. Yoon sets the scene: a blindfolded man juggles the shoes of the children, and Yohan shares his chocolate, the taste of which reminds him of the first time he ever tasted chocolate, in the American prison camp. This is followed by a sudden and overwhelming merging of past and present: "He waited, though what he was waiting for he was no longer sure of. His legs grew heavy, he felt his palms settle into the grass, and he imagined himself sinking, his body falling into the earth until the sea claimed him and there was nothing left, no evidence of him." On the heels of the corporeal detail come his more guarded thoughts: "He watched the ends of the scarf swing behind the blindfolded juggler. He thought of forests. High canopies. A river. A hand on his elbow." *Forests, high canopies, a river, a hand on his elbow*—once again, Yohan gestures offstage, and one has the sense that here is a person who keeps secrets not only from us but maybe even from himself.

Comyns's Alice and Yoon's Yohan offer us examples of characters who elude us just enough. The question of how much information to withhold about a character, particularly in a first-person narration, is tricky and case-specific. In every case, however, it's useful to ask, What is the effect of the withholding? Does it yield something generative in relation to character? Or is it an effort to drum up surface-level suspense, whose effect may be experienced as exactly that, effortful, and cosmetic, rather than as true dramatic tension? In a novel about an abused girl and a novel about a laconic refugee of war, these secrets are especially crucial as a means of ensuring the characters aren't limited to, or reduced by, their circumstance. Their secrets make them a bit messy, as though their authors have scribbled outside the lines, and that's a good thing. In *Aspects of the Novel*, Forster writes that a character "is real when the novelist knows everything about it. He may not choose to tell us all he knows—many of the facts, even of the kind we call obvious, may be hidden. But he will give us the feeling that though the character has not been explained, it is explicable, and we get from this a reality of a kind we can never get in daily life." It may sometimes be true that an author knows the secrets of his or her secret lives, but there is part of me that likes to think that the most potent characters become enough of a force to break free not only of the constraints of the narrative but also of the constraints of his or her creator.

Those Vivian Maier self-portraits are dated—1953 to 1971—except for those with no date at all. She is not always a shadow. There she is, tall, startling, beautiful, reflected in a silver platter in an antique store, in a hub-cap, in a bathroom whose mirrors extend her into infin-ity. There, reflected in a store window, a little girl (her charge?) hamming it up beside her; there, in another store window, the reflection of two women in her skirt, as though they've taken refuge there. There's only one where she's smiling, reflected in a full-length mirror being hoisted out of a Dumpster by a man whose face you cannot see. There's no getting to the bottom of her.

Mystery in Character (*Continued*): The Uses of Discomfort

What about the sort of character whose mystery grows out of contradiction, incongruity, irrationality? Who makes us wonder, even as we recognize some part of ourselves in the mess, why did that character *do* that? Many of these sorts of characters fall into that fraught category du jour, *unlikable*. Lurking behind those euphemistic character categories, "likable" and "unlikable," are those big aesthetic questions I mentioned earlier: *What do we want art to be? What do we want it to do?*

In addition to not ascribing the status of art to something that does one thing or is purely functional or is only a morality tale or only gets us off, I'm guessing we also don't ascribe it to stories that only reassure us, that serve as a flattering mirror or a kind of "selfie," as Rebecca Mead wrote in her *New Yorker* article "The Scourge of 'Relatability.'" Relatability is likability's twin, or at least its first cousin, a part of that happy family Tolstoy describes as being like every other happy family, which is to say nonexistent and without a lot of traction in the way of dramatic material. Like those happy families, characters who are only likable don't offer the labyrinthine intricacies characters require to become the "People" and "People (*Continued*)" of whom Forster spoke so fondly. The demand for likability is dangerous. It's a conversation stopper, and we need conversations, in so-called real life and in fiction.

The role that fiction, and particularly its ethereal quality of mystery, plays in political struggle is sometimes cast as, at best, negligible and, if the defunding of the humanities is any indication, at worst a luxury we can't afford. But fiction is an act of empathy and, increasingly these days, empathy can feel like a radical act. Where you direct your empathy, where you cultivate your reader's empathy, has meaning and motive. In his *Poetics*, Aristotle writes that the historian is concerned with "what has happened," whereas the poet is more concerned with "the kind of thing that would happen." This argument concerns the usefulness of the imagination in navigating the world and understanding ourselves in relation to it, and it suggests that art has something to offer us about the past—and so the present—that might run alongside history. Part of what art offers us is the variety of mystery that presses us up against brutal contradictions, that respects facts but features feeling in order to navigate the unsayable.

At the time of this writing, we are not so far from the 2014 police killing of Michael Brown in Ferguson,

Missouri; from the 2015 death of Freddie Gray in the back of a police transport van in Baltimore, Maryland; from the 2015 death of Sandra Bland in a jail cell in Waller County, Texas; from the 2016 fatal shooting of Philando Castile by a police officer in Falcon Heights, Minnesota, live-streamed on Facebook by his girl-friend, Diamond Reynolds, her four-year-old daughter a witness from the backseat of the car. Look at track-ing sites such as Mapping Police Violence (mapping policeviolence.org) to see how excruciatingly incom-plete this list is; to see that many other black people have been killed by the police since then. Since I wrote this sentence; and since right now, and now, and now. An urgent public conversation about white suprem-acy, systemic racism, and the murder of black people was centuries overdue. Ta-Nehisi Coates, in his letter to his son, *Between the World and Me*, speaks to the problem of the idea of race itself: "Americans believe in the reality of 'race' as a defined, indubitable feature of the natural world. Racism—the need to ascribe bone-deep features to people and then humiliate, reduce, and destroy them—inevitably follows from this inalterable condition. . . . But race is the child of racism, not the fa-ther. And the process of naming 'the people' has never been a matter of genealogy and physiognomy so much as one of hierarchy."

After Lionel Shriver's now infamous keynote address,

"Fiction and Identity Politics," at the 2016 Brisbane Writers Festival (where, in a superhuman feat of tone deafness, she railed against the legitimacy of "cultural appropriation" as a critique while wearing a sombrero), Kaitlyn Greenidge wrote an op-ed in the *New York Times* called "Who Gets to Write What?" in which she argued for the depth of feeling necessary to fashion characters different from ourselves. She writes, "Imagine the better, stronger fiction that could be produced if writers took this challenge to stretch and grow one's imagination, to afford the same depth of humanity and interest and nuance to characters who look like them as characters who don't, to take those stories seriously and actually think about power when writing—how much further fiction could go as an art." Greenidge cites Toni Morrison's comment about anti-PC backlash, from a 1994 interview with Claudia Dreifus: "What I think the political correctness debate is really about is the power to be able to define. The definers want the power to name. And the defined are now taking that power away from them." To my ear, among the things Greenidge is meditating on, and advocating for, are radical empathy and a respect for mystery. That land of Un: unclenching, unknotting, unknowing. Part of creating complex characters is understanding what we don't understand, proceeding with humility and care. "There is the power of rendering another's perspective, which is not your own," writes Greenidge. "There is the adage 'Don't punch down,' which sits like the shiny red lever of a fire alarm, irresistible for some writers who wish to pull it."

Not punching down can work a lot of different ways on the page. Sometimes it means not taking the easy shot when it comes to depicting those we might consider beyond redemption, from whom we want to distance ourselves completely. Take, for example, the first-person narrator in Eudora Welty's 1963 story "Where Is the Voice Coming From?," a fictional version of Medgar Evers's assassin, Byron De La Beckwith, composed on the day of the murder. Welty was raised in Jackson, Mississippi, about eighty miles from Beckwith's hometown of Greenwood. "What I was writing about really was that world of hate I felt I had grown up with," she said in an interview with William F. Buckley, "and I felt I could speak as someone who knew it." Still, the title of the story is not a question with any one answer. That is the project of the story, to dwell in a place where there are no answers at all; instead it offers us terrifying proximity to a character whose voice most of us would prefer *not* to imagine. The story imagines an event that should be unimaginable, that should be unbearable, but is, unfortunately, neither of those things. If it were unimaginable, then the murder of Evers, and all of the murders leading up to it, wouldn't have happened; if the murder of black people were unbearable,

we'd all be dead. The story's formal insistence on proximity through a first-person narration is what makes it
so powerful.

"I says to my wife, 'You can reach and turn it off.
You don't have to set and look at a black nigger face
no longer than you want to, or listen to what you don't
want to hear. It's still a free country.'" This is the scorch-
ing beginning from the heart of the narrator's rage.
There is the shock of the n-word. There is the venom-
ous insecurity (*turn it off*). Shot, too, out of the cannon
of Welty's anger and anguish over Evers's murder, the
story bears traces of the cannon powder as she shows
her hand a bit. That Welty not only could imagine the
mind of this man but that she did imagine it requires
artistic rigor, of the sort that might be required of a
contemporary writer to imagine the mind of Dylann
Storm Roof when the Reverend Clementa Pinkney wel-
comed Roof, inviting him to sit down with the prayer
circle at an AME church in Charleston in June 2015.
The radical empathy of creating character requires
rigor no matter whose consciousness you're imagining;
it requires a combination of hard-won knowledge and
the mystery of all you will never know in an effort to
move beyond the story of what happened to the story
of the things that can happen.

That Beckwith has a private life may seem obvious,
but to be stuffed into the too-tight suit of this first-

person narration is also to be stuffed inside the character's rage and insecurity, the shock of the racist epithet, and Welty's own rage. It's not comfortable and that's the point. And then there's the affecting music of the voice. In her essay "Writing Short Stories," Flannery O'Connor writes, "A great deal of the Southern writer's work is done for him before he begins, because our history lives in our talk." The narrator, upon shooting Roland Summers, the fictional version of Evers, tells us, "Something darker than him, like the wings of a bird, spread on his back and pulled him down. He climbed up once, like a man under bad claws, and like just blood could weigh a ton he walked with it on his back to better light. Didn't get no further than his door. And fell to stay." In this slippery series of sentences, the narrator distances himself from the murder through lyricism. The violence is almost beautiful, but with *something darker*, Welty indicts not only the narrator but also a society in which white privilege rules, the same society in which Beckwith flourished, the place from which Welty writes. Implicit in this phrasing is a question: Are you complicit with a rigged system where some people have privilege and power and others do not? It has an effect akin to the parable David Foster Wallace made reference to in his 2005 Kenyon graduation speech that became an Internet sensation:

> There are these two young fish swimming along, and
> they happen to meet an older fish swimming the
> other way, who nods at them and says, "Morning,
> boys. How's the water?" And the two young fish swim
> on for a bit, and then eventually one of them looks
> over at the other and goes, "What the hell is water?"

Welty's story may be born from rage and anguish, but it doesn't end there. If it's to succeed it has to slip us into the *I* of a man we don't want to be anywhere near, whom we don't even want to know, and then take us even further, even deeper, into the mystery and contradiction of the character's humanity. Here's where it ends: "So I reach me down my old guitar off the nail in the wall. 'Cause I've got my guitar, what I've held on to from way back when, and I never dropped that, never lost or forgot it, never hocked it but to get it again, never give it away, and I set in my chair, with nobody home but me, and I start to play, and sing a-Down. And sing a-down, down, down, down. Sing a-down, down, down, down. Down." Where is the voice coming from? From traditions so deeply entrenched he can't see them. (*What the hell is water?*) From a place so isolated he can't see how much sorrow he's caused, or how isolated he is. We understand the direction in which he is headed because of the repetition in the lyrics; and, in case we think this has nothing to do with us, implied with his downward spiral is—thanks to the earlier reference to the larger *something darker*—the country's. There's the mystery inherent in the inimitable approximation of self of this particular character, singing this eerie, portentous song. It leaves one with a feeling that isn't pure anger or pure anguish but that includes both and also a feeling that's difficult to articulate, a feeling Welty has drawn our attention to with the story, something that requires our desperate attention.

J. M. Coetzee's novel *Waiting for the Barbarians* is a fierce, beautifully compressed novel interested in the soporific effects of Empire on what might be described as Empire's middle management. One of the questions the novel poses is, What happens when one of Empire's middle managers is shaken awake out of his stupor? *Empire? What the hell is Empire?* The novel is part allegory. We're in an outpost of an un-identified Empire in an unnamed country where an unnamed magistrate has been dozily holding down the fort against so-called barbarians who, like the imaginary barbarians in the C. P. Cavafy poem to which Coetzee's title makes reference, are always on the verge of arrival. The last stanza of Cavafy's poem reads, "Now what's going to happen to us without bar-barians? / Those people were a kind of solution." The barbarians in the poem, and in Coetzee's novel, are the all-too-convenient Other.

Waiting for the Barbarians was published in 1980, when Coetzee, a South African writer, was still living in South Africa and apartheid was still the law of the land. Nearly two decades later, Coetzee published *Disgrace*, after which he left South Africa for Australia and never returned. *Disgrace* might be considered a postapartheid sequel to *Waiting for the Barbarians*; it takes the allegorical blueprint and gets excruciatingly specific about time and place. We're in postapartheid South Africa, and our protagonist is a white South African with a name, David Lurie, whose disgrace is the sort of disgrace that keeps on giving (both personal and political, part self-inflicted and part inevitable tragic backlash of the apartheid regime). I mention *Disgrace* because David Lurie is another good example of mystery in character that takes the form of contradiction, a guy who is relentlessly intractable and enraging and who will never, ever apologize for it, even if, as Coetzee does, you set him on fire. If you haven't already, go read *Disgrace*. Have a lot of episodes of *The Prancing Elites* (or whatever your version of joyful solace is) on hand to watch in between chapters.

But I want to talk about *Waiting for the Barbarians* because my hunch is that it's where *Disgrace* began. Like *Disgrace*, *Waiting for the Barbarians* is a novel about complicity, but unlike *Disgrace*, where David Lurie's bad behavior is in your face from the start, the unnamed magistrate's bad behavior sneaks up on you.

The novel's moral allegory contains a built-in mystery. As Coetzee himself commented, "The Magistrate and the girl could as well be Russian and Kirghiz, or Han and Mongol, or Turk and Arab, or Arab and Berber." Rather than *What is happening in South Africa?* the book's question is *What is happening in any civilization where the arbitrary distinction between the civilized and the barbarian is made?* It's a roving question, in search of *and* finding. It will find you too. Coetzee cuts the generic expansiveness with the claustrophobically intimate, whispered, present-tense confession of the first-person narration.

In this pathetic, perverse, cringingly human first-person narrator, the second and third layers of mystery reside. There's the question of who this guy is, and there's the question of why he's doing what he's doing. The tale that our narrator, the unnamed magistrate, unfolds is this: A bureaucrat, Colonel Joll, is sent by the Third Bureau, the Empire's secret service, because there have been rumors that the so-called barbarians for whom everyone has been waiting are going to mutiny. Interrogations of prisoners begin, according to the methods of the Third Bureau as explained by Colonel Joll: "First I get lies, you see—this is what happens—first lies, then pressure, then more lies, then more pressure, then the break, then more pressure, then the truth." At the time of the book's publication in the early 1980s, the Third Bureau might have put a reader in mind of the South African secret police or the Stasi or the KGB; post 9/11, they will also call to mind the use of torture by the United States under the auspices of the "war on terror." "I did not mean to get embroiled in this," the narrator tells us. "I am a country magistrate, a responsible official in the service of the Empire, serving out my days on this lazy frontier, waiting to retire." The narrator prefers to understand himself as a helpless cog in the machine of Empire, but the story is interested in the choice he has made to see himself as helpless. How does that happen? Until the arrival of Colonel Joll, the magistrate has been collecting taxes, supervising junior officers, keeping an eye on trade, and presiding over the court. It's a novel about what it means to choose not to see: "For the rest I watch the sun rise and set, eat and sleep and am content." See no evil. It is a novel about what it means to choose not to hear: "Of the screaming which people afterwards claim to have heard from the granary, I hear nothing." Hear no evil. And the narrator talks a good game too.

The novel would not succeed if we could hold ourselves apart from the experience of the magistrate, if we could avoid rubbing up against his humanity. With the magistrate, one of the keys to cultivating the reader's empathy is that first-person, present-tense narration whose gradual descent into complicity with a corrupt and murderous regime is a little like (I'm guessing) being gently choked by a python: vaguely cozy at first and then the squeeze and then it's too late.

The first step in winding the python around the reader's neck is, as with any novel, the first paragraph:

> I have never seen anything like it: two little discs of glass suspended in front of his eyes in loops of wire. Is he blind? I could understand it if he wanted to hide blind eyes. But he is not blind. The discs are dark, they look opaque from the outside, but he can see through them. He tells me they are a new invention. "They protect one's eyes against the glare of the sun," he says. "You would find them useful out here in the desert. They save one from squinting all the time. One has fewer headaches. Look." He touches the corners of his eyes lightly. "No wrinkles." He replaces the glasses. It is true. He has the skin of a younger man. "At home everyone wears them."

These "two little discs of glass suspended in front of his eyes in loops of wire" are, of course, sunglasses. "Loops of wire" will appear later in the novel as instruments of torture and control, looped through the cheeks of prisoners. Reading the novel the first time through, without knowing what's to come, anyone might finish this paragraph with a queasy, disoriented feeling, paralleling the narrator's own feeling at the sight of Colonel Joll; and then there you and the narrator are, conjoined in that queasy disorientation. In a novel occupied with seeing and willed blindness, the beginning does what all good beginnings should, introduces us to the essential ideas of the novel. *Is he blind?* Well, morally speaking, yes. And so, we gradually come to learn, is the magistrate.

We begin with an *I* whose innocence is featured (*two little discs of glass. . . . Is he blind?*), who has been, so he tells us, watching the sun rise and set, eating and sleeping, and otherwise being content. An *I* who becomes appropriately angry when Colonel Joll begins interrogating and torturing prisoners. An *I* who writes angry letters to the Third Bureau objecting. But, as it turns out, the first two prisoners were captured and imprisoned by him, and he never sends those angry, objecting letters. I say *him* and *he* but there you are, sunk deep in that same *I*, but now *I* is doing the imprisoning; *I* is not sending those angry, objecting letters. We soon learn that the narrator has been sleeping with so many of the scullery maids that it's a joke among the soldiers: "From the kitchen to the Magistrate's bed in sixteen easy steps." Soon after we learn of this joke, he begins an affair with a so-called barbarian girl (he refers to her throughout as a "girl," though it's unclear how old she is). The affair is pretty creepy: he bathes her and questions her about the interrogations she endured with Colonel Joll's men when she first arrived at the outpost, resulting in her scars and broken feet. "I behave in some ways like a lover—I undress her, I bathe her, I stroke her, I sleep beside her," the narrator tells us, "—but I might equally well tie her to a chair and beat her." Their encounters end when he is plunged into a dreamless, coma-like sleep, an oblivion described as "dreamless spells . . . like death to me, or enchantment, blank, outside time." Pretty sexy. We eventually learn that she is the daughter of one of the prisoners who died after an interrogation, though the magistrate can't remember her arrival as a prisoner. She is among the things the magistrate doesn't really see. Eventually, guilt-ridden and frustrated, he decides to return her to her people, though whether she has any actual family left is un- likely. Still, he heads out, handing her off to men in the middle of the desert, after which Colonel Joll accuses him of consorting with the enemy.

And then the story flips. The magistrate finds him- self locked in the cell where he once locked prisoners, undergoing the same interrogations. Agents of the Third Bureau "came to [his] cell to show [him] the meaning of humanity, and in the space of an hour they showed [him] a great deal."

What brought the magistrate to this moment? Where did he come from, for example? How did he end up at his post in the first place? What was his childhood like? Coetzee doesn't tell us. What the narrator wants from the barbarian girl is blatantly obvious—"Is it she I want or the traces of a history her body bears?"—and totally unclear. Part of what happens between them can be accounted for by the perils of power combined with sexual impulse, even though the magistrate's body is a mystery to himself. He describes his erection as "an arrow growing out of me, pointing nowhere" and wonders "why one part of my body, with its unreasonable cravings and false promises, should be heeded over any other as a channel of desire. Sometimes my sex seemed to me another being entirely, a stupid animal living parasitically upon me, swelling and dwindling according to autonomous appetites, anchored to my flesh with claws I could not detach." The novel can seem, at times, enamored of the ways that men are culturally hardwired to dominate women, as well as the uses of sexual dominance as another tool in the colonizer's tool kit. But the unsettling power of the novel derives from our being permitted to see the ways in which the magistrate is unaware of his own biases, so buried are they. He can't see the way his hard-on has grown, so to speak, out of his desire to dominate this woman, but Coetzee allows us to see the magistrate's blind spot.

The aspect of the relationship that mystifies the magistrate, and us, is delivered most palpably in his dreams, which share some of the qualities of the hypnotized state—performative and magically transporting. Dreams that are too much of either can be a death knell in fiction. When the proper balance is struck, however, they can provide an effective otherworldly randomness, offering a glimpse into the strange stew of a character's subconscious desires where two plus two rarely equals four. In the magistrate's dreams about the girl (who when she was around, remember, left him dream*less*), she is a shape-shifter, changing sex and size and age; in most of the dreams, she's not only out of reach, she's turned her back on him. Even in his dreams, he cannot see her. The dreams are surreal pockets that serve a useful structural purpose, creating momentum as they move us toward the very end of the novel. In the final scene, the magistrate finds himself in the barracks yard, which is where the final dream of the girl takes place. It is snowing, as in the dream. Rather than providing punctuation for the dream, however, the ending leaves him, and us, with a question: "This is not the scene I dreamed of. Like much else nowadays I leave it feeling stupid, like a man who lost his way long ago but presses on along a road that may lead nowhere."

He's not stupid, this guy, and this incongruity—an intelligent man who does stupid things—is part of the mystery baked into his character (a mystery, I'm sure I don't need to remind you, is baked into humanity). As his fate unfolds, he is able to articulate all of his wrong turns. He is even able to articulate his moral confusion, though perhaps not the underlying reasons for his creepy behavior. Coetzee creates mystery around the character by withholding and then revealing certain key details. The element of mystery in the magistrate's character comes from his limited understanding of all that is unfolding around him in the name of Empire and of his place in it. Sometimes, this novel demonstrates, mystery relies on showing the reader all of your cards. The magistrate is trapped by himself and, because we have been drawn into and immersed in his first-person perspective, we are trapped too, made to squirm as we contemplate alongside him the puzzle of history and the way we fail as human beings and cannot escape history, much as we might like to.

What is history anyway? Another of the novel's big questions. Does it start with the written word? One of the magistrate's hobbies before the arrival of Colonel Joll is excavating the ruins of whatever culture was destroyed before the Empire arrived, in which he discovers archaic writing on poplar slips, which he tries to decipher but cannot. History doesn't rely merely on what is recorded but also on whether what is recorded is legible and deemed worthy and important by those with power. Near the end of the novel—after the magistrate has been stripped of his post, beaten until he is reduced to a body in pain, and then publicly humiliated for good measure, after he has nothing else to lose—still when he sits down to make a record for posterity, to compose, in effect, *history*, this is what he writes: "No one who paid a visit to this oasis . . . failed to be struck by the charm of life here." He wants to be outside of history but he is drowning in it. *What the hell is water?*

"To the last we will have learned nothing," he tells us. There is a brutal, stubborn nihilism to the novel, and to the magistrate, but there is also a pervasive sense of wanting to know or at least a wish to think about what we can't know. How should one live in relation to history, about which we have some (but never enough) information? How does one avoid falling into a stupor that prevents seeing or hearing or otherwise not paying attention until it is much too late? The novel is a pebble dropped into a vast sea, and the questions keep rippling outward. Why does a person enter into time in this or that period of history, into this or that body, into this or that skin? One could ponder these questions for a lifetime. People have, they do, they will. The novel's final note of uncertainty suggests an interest in something beyond nihilism. Or maybe in addition to. Like one of the poplar slips whose archaic writing the magistrate tries to decipher, this novel is an enigmatic envoy from the past whose efforts at communication are a small act of hope. *See this. Hear this. Speak of this.*

Jane Bowles's story "Camp Cataract" offers characters who confound in a manner quite different from Coetzee's. Bowles created absurd, topsy-turvy fictional worlds featuring odd, eccentric characters whom she dignified by treating as neither odd nor eccentric. There is a gloriously outrageous quality to this story from a neglected writer whose subversive characters thrashed against the confines of the conventional.

"Camp Cataract" might be described as a story about a family history of mental illness, but more than that—and this feature runs through Bowles's body of work—it is empathetic toward, and celebratory of, queerness. "Queerness" in all senses of that word, in the old-fashioned sense of strange or odd or unconventional, and as the word has been adopted in the more political sense. The story is about the very idea of incongruity and its importance in waking us from our stupor, and the electricity of the characters derives from Bowles's signature element of surprise.

The premise of "Camp Cataract" is this: there are

four sisters—the most stable sister (unnamed, perhaps, because of that stability) who exists offstage;
Evelyn, the sister who claims she is the most stable;
and the third and fourth sisters, whom Evelyn charac-
terizes thusly: "One of them [Harriet] is so crazy that
she must live in a cabin for her nerves at *my* expense,
and the other one [Sadie] is planning to go crazy deliberately and behind my back." The story begins in-
scene with Harriet in her cabin at Camp Cataract, part
asylum, part rustic tourist destination whose library
includes, inexplicably, oeuvres such as *The Growth
and Development of the Texas Oil Companies*. With
Harriet is her main source of companionship at Camp
Cataract, a tough waitress named Beryl, who has an
obsessive crush on Harriet, having "recorded in her
mind entire passages of Harriet's monologues out
of love for her friend, although she felt no curiosity
concerning the material she had gathered." Harriet is
reading a letter from her sister Sadie, with whom she
has what might be described in today's parlance as a
codependent relationship. "I wish they didn't think you
needed to go to Camp Cataract because of your spells,"
Sadie writes poignantly. "Haven't I always tended
you when you had them?" There's often a maverick
tonal weather in a Jane Bowles story—cloudy with a
chance of the apocalypse—and "Camp Cataract" is no
exception.

"Everything that goes on between us goes on under-cover," Harriet says of her relationship with Sadie. In fact, *everything* that goes on with Sadie goes on under-cover; she's disguised even to herself. Bowles is less interested in analyzing this quality, or pathologizing it; what interests her more is the poignant vaudeville of siblinghood and, more broadly, the human condi-tion. There's a description of the dining room table in the home of Evelyn—"much too wide for the small oblong-shaped room"—that serves as an apt descrip-tion of these characters and their uneasy relationship to the conventional world. And the shape of the table, as all seemingly ill-fitting things do, shows us the shape of the room.

The letter Harriet receives sets in motion the present action of the story: Sadie sneaks off to Camp Cataract to retrieve Harriet, or so it seems. In a letter to Harriet, Sadie writes of her fear of nomads and wanderlust, in-sinuating that Harriet might be such a nomad herself. Over the course of the story, however, there's a photo-negative effect in which what was once dark becomes light and what was once light becomes dark. Sadie is clearly the one overcome by a fatal variety of wander-lust, the sort that leads, quite literally as we'll discover, to wandering right over the edge. This is set in motion by an interaction with the souvenir booth vendor who tends the booth near the cataract for which the camp is named. The Irish vendor's work outfit includes the full war regalia of a cartoon version of an Indian chief and full redface, but in the penultimate scene of the story, Sadie notices the discrepancy between the freckled white of the vendor's hand and the painted-on red color of his face (he had neglected to paint his hands that day). "What was it? She was tormented by the sight of an incongruity she couldn't name." The fraudulent souvenir booth vendor becomes a mirror for Sadie's own confusion. Only by throwing herself into the abyss of the cataract can she find relief from the torment of her own incongruity. Sadie, it turns out, is the one for whom the world is unbearable.

Sadie is someone on whom everything is lost. It doesn't occur to her, for example, "that a connection might exist between her present dismal state and the mission she had come to fulfill at Camp Cataract." She is a tangle of contradictions—she is, for example, wily without understanding her own wiliness: "Although Sadie was neither sly nor tricky, but on the contrary profoundly sincere and ingenuous, she schemed unconsciously." Ultimately, we don't get much in the way of explanation for Sadie's despair beyond her tangled but true affection for Harriet and a vague allusion to the family's history of mental illness. But this is how Bowles wants it. She is not interested in having Sadie name the tormenting incongruity; nor is Bowles interested in naming it herself. She is directing our attention elsewhere.

The pleasure in this story has everything to do with the unexpected, which resides in the off-the-wallness of Harriet. "Don't you imagine that just because I'm a bit peculiar and different from the others, that I'm not fussy about my life," she says; she makes declarations à propos of not much (she hates industrialization!); she likes to "practice imagination for an hour or two" each morning. And in the sweet, unexamined, hesitant nomadism of Sadie—poor Sadie!—whose self-realization requires self-destruction. Bowles's palpable affection for these sisters—unmarried, eccentric, too wide for the oblong-shaped room of the world—has to do with their relentless, often hilarious, peculiarity and their love for one another.

Though the story's not much occupied with plot, it is still quite shapely—that photonegative effect is punctuated by the pivot when Sadie has her encounter with the souvenir booth vendor. Ultimately, though, it is the defiant oddness, the consistent inconsistency, of these characters, their resistance to answering their own questions, never mind ours, that lights them up on the page.

It's important to note the difference between bizarre characterizations for their own sake and the variety of bizarre characterization that yields something stranger and deeper. As with most things in fiction, it's a question of effect. Is a bizarre character, and the mystery surrounding that character, being generated for look-at-me-Ma show, or is it doing something that leads to generative mystery? That fourth and forgotten unnamed sister in "Camp Cataract" may hold a key. Referred to only as "the more affluent sister," she doesn't merit a name, as Sadie and Harriet and Evelyn do, precisely because it is with Sadie and Harriet and Evelyn that the dramatic possibilities of struggle lie. It's not merely that the named sisters are weird; they press themselves against the world. They flail and that flailing creates tension, which is tucked away inside the very rhythm of Bowles's sentences and in the cracked way the characters speak. This tension urges the reader ever forward.

If ruthless oddness is what illuminates Bowles's sisters, it is the thing that sets Shirley Jackson's delectably disturbing Merricat aflame in Jackson's fleet novel *We Have Always Lived in the Castle*. This was Jackson's last novel and, as with Bowles's "Camp Cataract," it is uncompromising. Here is the opening paragraph:

> My name is Mary Katherine Blackwood. I am eighteen years old, and I live with my sister Constance. I have often thought that with any luck at all I could have been born a werewolf, because the two middle

fingers on both my hands are the same length, but
I have had to be content with what I had. I dislike
washing myself, and dogs, and noise. I like my sister
Constance, and Richard Plantagenet, and *Amanita
phalloides*, the death-cup mushroom. Everyone else
in my family is dead.

Spoiler alert. Everyone else in her family is dead
because she *killed* them. Jackson never gives us a reason for Merricat's homicidal impulses. Often Merricat
imagines wishing other people dead, just so she can walk
on their bodies. She is full of superstitions—repeating
talismanic phrases to herself, making pronouncements
such as that Thursday is her "most powerful day," nail-
ing books to trees, and burying her dolls. She has fash-
ioned a world of magical spells and obsessive rituals
to fend off . . . what, exactly? The worst has happened.
All she wants is to live with her long-suffering sister Constance, who doesn't allow Merricat to prepare
other people's foods (because she, you know, poisoned
the whole family), while shielding her as best she can
from yet another of Shirley Jackson's unruly mobs of
villagers looking for the slightest excuse to stone someone to death. "Slowly," Merricat tells us from the creepy
house on the hill where she's holed up with Constance,
"the pattern of our days grew, and shaped itself into a
happy life."

She's a hard sell if likability is the measure, and you definitely wouldn't want to invite her to dinner. She's not going to provide a role model for how to live, and if you're reading to find a friend, she's not it. So what is Jackson offering us instead? Before you know it, you've lost track of the forest for the trees (to which Merricat's nailed all those books). Jackson seduces you with Merricat's strange, jump-cut way of speaking, and soon you're cocooned in the sticky logic of Merricat's world. You suspect from the start that she's the murderess (so I feel less bad for spoiling it for you). But her murderousness is not the main attraction here. The why of it all is not what interests Jackson. It's not that the novel is uninterested in morality; it's just much more interested in the music of Merricat's voice. An eerie sensibility roils underneath its surface, the twisted song of a feral, childish young woman who has committed the thing most of us wouldn't even cop to fantasizing about. A twist on the twisted. A Philip Larkin poem, squared: "They fuck you up, your mum and dad." So poison them.

In Merricat, Jackson has created an opportunity for us to dwell in the presence of a character who is an absurd amplification of our unspoken desires. She takes us to a place we might not otherwise even know how to get to and makes us look. Merricat is troubling, frightening, thrilling, and utterly perplexing. Why did she do that? Merricat, to put it mildly, does not behave the way we might expect or want her to. But this isn't about us, is it? Jackson brings us into the presence of Merricat's mystery.

Fiction is a rare opportunity, an occasion, for us to be led out on a perch outside the cage of self for a little bit. We are enticed onto that perch by characters (like Welty's narrator) who force us to reckon with their evil and in so doing quite possibly with our own; who enrage and frustrate us as Coetzee's unnamed magistrate does; who poke and prod us with their pointed illogicality as Bowles's splendiferously bizarre pair of sisters do; who horrify us and get under our skin as Merricat does. Hands steady on Kafka's axe, these characters plunge the axe into our frozen souls.

The Mystery in Imagery

Alongside the secret lives of characters are the secret lives of images. Images transform the random into the resonant, the abstract into the concrete; they transform the murkily mysterious into the sort of mystery that invites the reader into its expansiveness. Joseph Conrad famously said that the great task of all writers is to make the reader see. In other words, a writer should take a reader beyond words *with* words. Counterintuitive as it may seem, Conrad's famous rallying cry crystallized for me when I finally overcame my resistance to graphic novels. I'm not proud that I resisted them; they annoyed me in a crotchety, old fogey sort of way. Such busy pages! They're giving me eyestrain! It's like trying to read and watch TV at the same time! I think I hurt my back! Then a friend became the fifth person to recommend Alison Bechdel's graphic memoir *Fun Home*. I've got a rule that says once five friends recommend a book I haven't read, it's time to read it.

Fun Home is, to boil it way down, the story of the difficult relationship between a daughter and her father. Throughout the book, the daughter wrestles with the timing of her father's death, which may or may not have been a suicide. The daughter, Bechdel, comes out as a lesbian to her parents, and, soon after, her father is hit by a truck and killed. As it turns out, the father has lived as a closeted gay man for many years, and when Bechdel comes out to her mother, her mother chooses that moment to unload all of her pent-up frustrations: You think *that's* hard? Try living with a repressed gay man for thirty years! To sum it up is to reduce it to melodrama, when it is magnificently nuanced. Bechdel's drawings have much in common with the eerie drawings of the mournful, giant-headed father in Bruno Schulz's *Street of Crocodiles* and the spooky, gothic quality of the woodcuts of Fritz Eichenberg in the 1944 limited edition of *Jane Eyre*. Bechdel's whimsical, beautiful drawings focus your attention on the story.

AND WHO KNOWS. PERHAPS HE DID.

There's one panel in *Fun Home* that I find especially spellbinding. It's a drawing of the deserted sliver of highway where the father was killed. The caption says simply: "And who knows. Perhaps he did." The highway is lumpy and cracked. It is desolate, and then on the other side of the road is a forest. At first the forest looks like a black blotch, but when you look closer, and the drawing makes you want to look closer, delicate shapes begin to emerge. There's a curved branch, fuzzy with foliage. There, the light shines through—an absence— and as a result, the branches and bushes make figures. A man running away, or is it a woman? You could look at the meticulously rendered forest for hours, and you would see more and more. The panel, whose words gesture to the father's possible suicide, enacts Paul Klee's observation from his 1920 *Creative Credo*: "Art does not reproduce the visible; rather it makes visible."

As a writer, Flannery O'Connor was obsessed with *making visible*. Images in her work become more mysterious the more narrative attention she pays to them. Her story "Good Country People" and its infamous wooden leg is a good example. In her essay "Writing Short Stories," O'Connor had this to say about that leg and the crucial distinction between building imagery from the inside out versus symbol planting: "If you want to say that the wooden leg is a symbol, you can say that. But it is a wooden leg first, and as a wooden leg it is absolutely necessary to the story. It has its place on the literal level of the story, but it operates in depth as well as on the surface."

The upshot of the plot of "Good Country People" is this: a boy masquerading as a Bible salesman steals the wooden leg of a woman named Joy who, with delicious bitterness, has renamed herself Hulga. Hulga professes, on the basis of much reading of Malebranche, to believe in nothing. The wooden leg gathers meaning as the story progresses; by the time the boy has lured Hulga into the hayloft; by the time he convinces her to unstrap the thing and hand it over; by the time he opens his suitcase and it turns out not to be full of Bibles after all but to be mostly empty save for some whiskey and a pack of cards; by the time all of this has come to pass, the leg has somehow come to suggest the woodenness of Hulga's own soul. It has a wooden quality, that soul, but it still swirls with mystery, as souls tend to do.

By the time the boy abandons Hulga up there in the hayloft, he's run off with something more than the leg. The theft takes the reader into the wild realm of the unparaphrasable. The poet and critic Yvor Winters once said of a poem that it should contain both paraphrasable and unparaphrasable content, and the same holds true of fiction. In "Good Country People," the paraphrasable is the mean joke of it all—a sneaky boy runs off with a miserable woman's wooden leg. The un-paraphrasable content is the ineffable feeling the reader is left with as the story's eye shifts from the boy escaping over the horizon to Hulga's cliché-driven mother and Mrs. Freeman, the woman who works on the farm and whose gaze is like receiving an X-ray without the protection of a lead vest. The story is about more than Hulga's loss; it is about this ecosystem of women the boy has disrupted, an ecosystem complicated by class, and race, and constructed identities, that divide between skin and what lies beneath, between how we present ourselves to ourselves and how we present ourselves to others and the chasm that often exists between those two presentations. The use of imagery—the repetition of that wooden leg—becomes part of the story's structure; it is how O'Connor leads us to that final portal, opening out rather than shutting the story down.

In his essay "Quickness," Italo Calvino describes what he calls *magic objects*: "the moment an object appears in a narrative, it is charged with a special force and becomes like the pole of a magnetic field, a knot in the network of invisible relationships." These magic objects are connecting forces, embodiment of abstract ideas. "Around the magic object there forms a kind of force field that is in fact the territory of the story itself. We might say that the magic object is an outward and visible sign that reveals the connection between people or between events." Imagery is a variety of magic object.

Hulga's wooden leg is a force field, an outward and visible sign, a place in the narrative where the big ideas can take up residence without being bossy, transforming the abstract idea of Hulga's wooden soul into something we can see, and hear, and experience sensually. At the memorial service for jazz saxophonist Ornette Coleman, musician Karl Berger remembered Coleman saying, "The less you think, the more your emotions will be fulfilled." In some ways, this is what we're after as fiction writers: less thinking, more emotion. We want the reader to think a little less and to feel more. This requires training the reader's gaze. To what would you like the reader to pay attention? And how do you draw attention to that thing? This requires attentiveness, patience, and making the reader see something until it becomes a part of the world of the story. In "Good Country People," O'Connor makes us see that leg from the start.

"Joy was her daughter, a large blonde girl who had an artificial leg." This is how we are introduced to Hulga née Joy. She's large; she's blonde; she's her mother's girl though she is thirty-two; and that artificial leg is as much a part of her as her large blondeness and her daughterhood. Hulga doesn't merely leave the kitchen table where her mother is eating her breakfast and gossiping with Mrs. Freeman about her fabulously trashy daughters. She *lumbers* into the bathroom. Her rage and that leg are one. Later, Hulga *stumps* into the kitchen. O'Connor rhymes Hulga's ugly name with what her mother considers her ugly-sounding wooden leg. The leg is Hulga's weapon and her defense.

O'Connor looks, and makes us look, at the leg over and over and over again. But it's not just the looking; it's the nature of the looking. O'Connor looks relentlessly at that leg until it seems no longer wooden but strangely alive. O'Connor once bragged about having come across the leg quite by accident, and while this assertion is as annoying as her claims to having written stories in a single draft, the accidental nature of the leg feels true. When you read the story, it's as if the leg was always there in the world and she just happened upon it.

To achieve the leg's already-thereness, O'Connor ensures it is studied by every character from every angle. Hulga's mother thinks of her daughter's artificial leg as tragic. She'd prefer her hulking woman-child progeny to be a cliché of a daughter, the "wheel behind the wheel," but the story makes it clear that Hulga's *lumbering, stumping* leg will not be drowned out by her mother's clichés. Mrs. Freeman, on the other hand, with her "special fondness for the details of secret infections, hidden deformities, assaults upon children," can't get enough of that leg. If it were up to her, she would abandon the chitchat about her trashy daughters if it meant getting to hear the gory details of Hulga's hunting accident one more time. O'Connor describes Mrs. Freeman's "beady steel-pointed eyes . . . penetrat[ing] far enough behind [Hulga's] face to reach some secret fact," which is also a good description of the story's gaze in relation to the leg. The story studies it with such intensity it's a wonder it doesn't spontaneously combust. This scrutiny happens even before the so-called Bible salesman darkens the story's door. When he does appear, the wooden leg is as much a part of the way things are as Mrs. Freeman standing in the kitchen every morning. The leg is not an idea, or an element of the story, or an image that will someday turn into a symbol. It just is. O'Connor has turned it into something important while also allowing it to recede and become part of the story's background.

Because the image becomes a structural part of the story rather than an ornamental one, in the climactic scene, in which the Bible salesman seduces Hulga, O'Connor baldly links the leg with Hulga's soul. "She took care of it as someone else would his soul, in private and almost with her own eyes turned away." The leg lifts off from the literal into the metaphysical. We've seen the leg through the mother's histrionic lens, through Mrs. Freeman's blood-and-guts lens of fascination, and we've seen the way Hulga can't even bear to look. Still, when Hulga surrenders her leg to the Bible salesman, O'Connor makes us look again: "The artificial limb, in a white sock and brown flat shoe, was bound in a heavy material like canvas and ended in an ugly jointure where it was attached to the stump." Here, the third-person narration, while somewhat aligned with the boy Bible salesman, pulls back for a brutally frank assessment. This object, as much a part of Hulga as her large-ness and her blondeness, this thing that Hulga cares for as she would her very soul, is ugly and fake, deflated and lifeless, but it has also, by this point, transcended its physicality. Poor Hulga. Like so many of O'Connor's protagonists, she's been stripped of everything, readied for her moment of grace. She's more naked than if she were actually naked. The boy disappears over the hill, and we are left with Hulga's "churning face"—churning with a nuanced anguish to which O'Connor has made us privy by making us look and look and look, until we arrive at this ending where know-it-all Hulga doesn't have all of the answers. And neither do we.

The imagery in Chris Abani's deceptively slim novella *Song for Night* is less magical object than grim *tableau vivant*. *Song for Night* is narrated by a fifteen-year-old West African boy with the unlikely name My Luck, three years into an unnamed civil war in an unnamed West African country. My Luck is a member of a unit of children trained by the rebels to use knives to defuse unmapped mines laid by federal troops and rebels alike. "What you hear is not my voice" is the first sentence My Luck *doesn't* speak as he regains consciousness after being separated from his platoon following a land mine explosion. He has undergone what is considered routine surgery, his vocal cords severed so that if he sets off a mine he won't distract his fellow soldiers with his screaming. Each chapter describes another gesture in the sign language the voiceless children have invented to communicate—"Imagination Is a Forefinger between the Eyes," for example. These chapter titles, often ironic and pointed, organize the story of My Luck's search for home.

Like the unnamed magistrate in Coetzee's *Waiting for the Barbarians*, My Luck is an archetypal character: this is what it's like to be a boy soldier in a West African war, to steal, rape, and kill, to watch your parents, your friends, your lover die. My Luck is at once archetypal and utterly himself. Abani's strategic use of imagery reflects My Luck back to us, cultivating mystery and complicating this boy soldier, allowing for the expanse of character in spite of his potentially heavy narrative armature.

While O'Connor's wooden leg works through repetition, Abani's mystery-generating images are impressionistic; in *Song for Night*, there are many such swift and potent images but there are two that are especially pivotal. The first occurs in memory. My Luck remembers seeing a group of men, women, and children, all maimed in some way by the war, gathered around a fire. Because first-person narration is usually all character all the time, what My Luck chooses to see and remember and the way he sees tell us a great deal about him:

> Someone had found a radio and it was tuned to a
> BBC World Service broadcast of Congolese highlife.
> There were a bunch of disabled children dancing
> in a circle. A young girl with one leg standing off to
> the side leaning on a stick made fun of the dancers.
> Challenged to do better, she laughed, threw the stick
> away, and jumped into the circle. She stood still for a
> moment as though she was getting her bearings,
> and then she began to move. Still balanced on one
> leg, her waist began a fierce gyration and her upper
> body moved the opposite way. Then like a crazy
> heron, she began to hop around, her waist and torso
> still shaking. She was an elemental force of nature.
> I couldn't take my eyes off her.

Here Abani and My Luck are restrained in deference to the image of the girl dancing, which allows the image to permeate the atmosphere of the story, conveying a dreamlike horror. The girl dancing contains the miracle of My Luck's own survival. Unlike Hulga, this girl has not been embittered by losing a leg, or hasn't *only* been embittered. And so, in the midst of violence and devastation, Abani attains the "lyric joy" Lionel Trilling once attributed to Isaac Babel's *The Red Cavalry*, and, like Babel, Abani frustrates any easy morality. The girl's "fierce gyration" contains rage, defiance, wildness, sexuality, the ecstatic, and something unpindownable. My Luck has exhibited these same qualities in the throes of the horror of war—he's still a teenage boy with all of the accompanying contradictory urges and emotions, as well as being a boy "lost in a war with a taste for rape" who, when he is forced to kill, hears "the juicy suck of flesh around a bayonet." The image of the dancing girl contains this contradictory mix—My Luck's adolescent sexuality, resilience, his brutal desire to endure, his own defiance—and allows him to elude us just enough. It is a pivotal moment in the novella. Images like this one are filled with the heat and electricity of the character observing them. They move the story forward on the level of the plot, as well as deeper into the dreamworld of the story, the rich, evocative, and mysterious territory of the subconscious.

The second pivotal image is inflected with all of the tribal myths My Luck's grandfather passed on to him, stories of the Igbo that Abani has made sure to tell us before we are presented with the image. The power and resonance of images depends on their strategic placement and timing; the reader needs to be prepared to receive them. For the bulk of the novella, My Luck walks beside a river down which corpses float "like a macabre regatta" and then, about halfway through the book, one corpse is brought into focus:

> A canoe drifts slowly past, a skeleton piloting it. . . .
>
> The canoe becomes entangled in some lilies growing in a green and white cluster, and though the tides are pulling at it, I know because the lilies are nodding their white heads in time that the boat will not dislodge. The skeleton sways back and forth with the boat's motion and it makes me think of an elaborate decoration on a Swiss clock. There is a cobweb between the bony arm and the empty chest.

My Luck has seen countless dead bodies at this point, many of them the bodies of people he loves, but he has never ritually mourned one. But something about this stranger's dead body compels him, maybe even its randomness: "Before I take the skeleton out of the canoe, I reach in and pull the cobweb gently free. I drape it over my head like a cap and then lift the skeleton with ease, careful not to shake any bones loose." This gesture, performed just before he lays the skeleton in a grave and plays "Taps" on his harmonica, isn't part of a formal ceremony; these are My Luck's own funereal rites, not those of the Igbo.

In an essay called "Ethics and the Narrative: The Human and Other," which appeared in *Witness*, Abani writes:

> This is what the art I make requires of me: that in order to have an honest conversation with a reader, I must reveal myself in all my vulnerability. Reveal myself, not in the sense of my autobiography, but in the sense of the deeper self, the one we keep too often hidden even from ourselves. This revelation is not designed to engender sympathy, or compassion, or even pity. These sentiments, while generous on the part of the reader, obscure the deeper intent, the deeper possibility. The point is to dissolve oneself into the journey of the protagonist, to face the most terrifying thing in narrative, the thing that has been at its heart since the earliest campfire and story. To dare ourselves to imagine, to conjure and then face all of our darkness and all of our light simultaneously. To stand in that liminal moment when we have no solid ground beneath us, no clear firmament above, when the ambiguity of our nature reveals what we are capable of, on both sides.

The image of grief—the cobweb cap—is surprising. In *Camera Lucida: Reflections on Photography*, Roland Barthes's meditation on the aesthetics of photography and an elegy for his mother, Barthes refers to the *studium*, which sets the scene, serving as a background, and the *punctum*, the element that ruptures the *studium* and pierces the viewer, "that accident which pricks." If the war-torn country through which My Luck wanders, including the river filled with dead bodies beside which he walks, comprises the *studium* of *Song for Night*, then the image of the cobweb cap is the *punctum*. The gesture with the cobweb surprises My Luck and so it surprises us too. In its precision, its intimacy, its futility, it startles you awake.

As I belatedly understood with Bechdel's *Fun Home*, Conrad's rallying cry—make the reader see!—applies not only to narratives built out of words but also to narratives built out of words and images. Of course it does. There is a long history of writers who incorporate photographic images into fictive narratives, beginning with *Bruges-la-Morte* (1892) by Belgian novelist Georges Rodenbach, who wove photographs of the decaying city through a tale of love gone wrong (*l'amour*, that tragic French homonym of *la mort*). The list of modern novelists, poets, and photographers who work in this tradition continues to grow—John Berger, Anne

Carson, Teju Cole, Daša Drndić, Aleksandar Hemon, Laird Hunt, Ben Lerner, Wright Morris, Nicholas Muellner, Michael Ondaatje, Claudia Rankine, Paisley Rekdal, and Catherine Taylor, to name only a few.

W. G. Sebald's alluringly melancholic hybrid novels are an essential part of this lineage. One of the many subjects of Sebald's work is mystery itself. A photograph, like a work of fiction, is a variety of portal, a door that opens onto what Walter Benjamin called in his 1931 essay "A Short History of Photography" a "tiny spark of accident, the here and now." An element of unpredictability relies on what the viewer brings to the photograph, in the same way a narrative relies on its engagement with its reader. The primary mechanism of the plot of Sebald's fourth novel, *The Rings of Saturn*, is indirection, and the uncaptioned photographic images, which often interrupt the narrative midsentence, add up to a fireworks display of tiny sparks of accident.

The novel follows the narrator in a walking tour of Suffolk, England, a walking tour circling the unspeakable—the Third Reich, the Holocaust, the devastation of war and genocide. Sebald's narrators frequently bear a striking resemblance to himself, and his novels frequently begin in a state of unease followed by acrobatic feats of associative digressions. In *The Rings of Saturn* the narrator starts by telling us that, a year after the walking tour, he had a breakdown: "At all events, in retrospect I became preoccupied not only with the unaccustomed sense of freedom but also with the paralysing horror that had come over me at various times when confronted with the traces of destruction, reaching far back into the past, that were evident even in that remote place. Perhaps it was because of this that, a year to the day after I began my tour, I was taken into hospital in Norwich in a state of almost total immobility."

The first photograph in the book is of a "colourless patch of sky framed in the window," taken, we are told, from the narrator's hospital bed. As the novel continues, there are snapshots of English port towns, now in economic ruin, reproductions of paintings, and scraps of journals and news clippings. Both the photographs and the reproductions have an amateurish quality: blurry, poorly reproduced, as if hastily photocopied. Sebald was in fact an accomplished photographer; you can see this in the photographs he uses in his other novels. The amateurish photographs in *The Rings of Saturn* increase the sense of intimacy between the reader and the narrator; one has the sense of the narrator handling the photographs, sifting through them, holding them up for our consideration. They are enigmatic and unsettling because they are just plain out of focus.

The photographs appear in the midst of paragraphs

that go on and on. And on. To the uninitiated Sebald can be a slog at first. Ask any of my students to whom I've assigned Sebald. I've read *The Rings of Saturn* five times now. This is not a brag. I'm telling you how many times it took before I began to get a handle on this book, before I felt included in its mystery. The compulsion to reread even when you feel thwarted, finding one's way into what one might call a difficult book, interests me. What is that about? It has, I think, to do with a seductive mystery; in Sebald's case, it has to do with the tug one feels into a narrative that deliberately, tantalizingly, encourages the question *Is this Sebald or isn't it?* This *is it or isn't it* leads you to the threshold of the photographs, another sphere of invention contained within an invention. You've stepped through one portal and then encounter others. The effect is dizzying.

The narrator walks the coastline of Lowestoft, encountering fishermen in pitched tents on a pebble beach, which leads him to a meditation on the dying out of the fishing industry and the fishermen themselves, as well as the pollution of the North Sea. Which leads to a meditation on the herring, and then herring fishing—"herring fishing regarded as a supreme example of mankind's struggle with the power of Nature." Then, having left the fishermen behind, he discovers himself on Benacre Broad Lake and remembers an article he once clipped from the *Eastern Daily Press* about the death of Major George Wyndham Le Strange, who lived nearby. The aptly named Le Strange served in the antitank regiment that liberated Bergen-Belsen at the end of World War II. Upon his death, he left his fortune to a housekeeper who was permitted to stay on after he returned from the war only if she agreed to dine with him in absolute silence, which she did. The images interspersed throughout the narrative of this particular leg of the narrator's journey include a photograph of an encampment on the beach, a photograph of men standing in the midst of an enormous haul of herring in Lowestoft, an illustration of a herring, a drawing of a luminous mountain, the newspaper clipping about Major Le Strange, and, finally, taking up two entire pages, a blurry photograph that is hard to make out at first. When you look closer, you realize it's a grisly photograph of the hundreds of dead prisoners murdered by the Nazis, discovered upon the liberation of Bergen-Belsen.

Somehow the walk along the Lowestoft coast has led us here. There is a fundamental physiological logic to it: the narrator's feet, one foot in front of the other, make contact with the earth and stir up the layers of history buried there. That he is quite literally walking through history is central to Sebald's enterprise. Of equal importance are the portals the images provide, in conjunction with the narration of the narrator's journey, onto the land of Un: uncertainty, unknowing, unfathomability. Of the fishermen's encampment on the beach, the narrator tells us, "They say it is rare for any of the fishermen to establish contact with his neighbour, for, although they all look eastward and see both the dusk and the dawn coming up over the horizon, and although they are all moved, I imagine, by the same unfathomable feelings, each of them is nonetheless quite alone." Of those herring and whether, as some natural historians optimistically suggest, they are free of pain and fear when they are killed, he tells us, "the truth is that we do not know what the herring feels." The shapes within the images themselves rhyme—the mass of dead herring, that strange luminous mountain, and the photograph of the dead at Bergen-Belsen—echoing a slanted rhyme in the narrator's heartbroken preoccupation with the mystery of catastrophe and devastation. Even as this fiercely erudite man connects the dots between staggeringly disparate parts of history, he is increasingly aware of how little we know, of how little we *can* know, in a lifetime. "We, the survivors [of history], see everything from above, see everything at once, and still we do not know how it was."

Sebald said of photographic images that they "militate against our capacity for discursive thinking." This is true, as well, of the sort of imagery in fiction built entirely out of words: O'Connor's wooden leg, Abani's cobweb mourning cap. Imagery in fiction defies logic. It defies conclusion. It is its own variety of spirit portraiture; around its crisp edges hover all sorts of ghosts. The ghosts of history, the ghosts of war, the ghosts of ourselves, the ghosts of things for which we have no name.

Looking Out, Looking In

Starting in 1947 with his painting *Wind from the Sea*, Andrew Wyeth, over the course of sixty years, made more than three hundred paintings whose subject is windows. Wyeth, better known for his realist paintings (think *Christina's World*) often said he preferred to be thought of as an abstractionist; a few years ago, there was an exhibition of his window paintings at the National Gallery of Art in Washington, DC, that lent some truth to this claim. In each of the paintings, the fixed, geometric shape of the window frames organizes, highlights, and otherwise contains something otherworldly and amorphous. The studies for many of the paintings were also hung in the exhibit side by side with the finished paintings. These studies have in them figures that have been painted over in the painting's final incarnation—the local boy who sits on a bench in front of a window in *The Vestry (Study for Off at Sea)*, for example, has been replaced with a single wire hanger in *Off at Sea*. His body has been absorbed into light and shadow, the window enlarged, drawing your gaze out to sea ("off at sea" refers to people lost at sea). *Spring Fed* (1967), a painting of a spring well inside a barn, contains a window that looks out onto an innocent field of cows, but Wyeth's father's death took place not far from that field, just around the corner of the painting. That potent sense of death just around the corner saturates many of these peopleless paintings—whether it's the lone lit-up window, a glowing star, in the otherwise dark universe of a house at night; or a window that reflects gathering storm clouds over the sea; or windows obscured by half shadow or curtains or glints of light.

The title of the exhibit, *Looking Out, Looking In*, is also a useful way of thinking about the way we experience mystery. "The expression of wonder stands for all that cannot be understood, that can scarcely be believed," Stephen Greenblatt writes in his book *Marvelous Possessions: The Wonder of the New World*, on the subject of how objects from the so-called New World exhibited in late-fifteenth-century and early-sixteenth-century cabinets of wonder blew the minds of Europe. "Someone witnesses something amazing, but what most matters takes place not 'out there' or along the receptive surfaces of the body where the self encounters the world, but deep within, at the vital, emotional center of the witness." Mystery and its attendant qualities of wonder and miracle rely on a combination of looking out and looking in.

When I saw the exhibit *Looking Out, Looking In*, I couldn't stop thinking about James Baldwin's 1957 short story "Sonny's Blues," a story full of windows. There are more than ten windows in the story, and each window serves as part of the story's architecture, and as a means of creating mystery. "Sonny's Blues" is epic in scope, and there's a lot to say, a lot that *has* been said, about this novelistic story, which acrobatically travels through crystal-clear convolutions in time. The story brings us into intimate proximity with the confessional voice of a narrator who is telling on himself with this account that carries him "some place [he] didn't want to go." Yet he is driven—by shame, by love, by rage, by grief—to tell us anyway.

Over the course of this story about the fraught relationship between two African American brothers—the narrator, an excruciatingly responsible, "square" (in the parlance of the time) algebra teacher, and his younger brother Sonny, a freewheeling, reckless heroin user and staggeringly talented jazz pianist—the narrator learns to see as opposed to merely look, to listen as opposed to merely hear, and to make room for the story for which he thought he had no room. This is the story, Sonny eventually explains, about how there is no way not to suffer: "But you try all kinds of ways to keep from drowning in it, to keep on top of it, and to make it seem—well, like *you*." The story encompasses the history of pervasive racism, the crushing weight of slavery and white supremacy, and simultaneously tells an intimate story of two brothers whose relationship and whose lives bear the brunt of that history. The voice of the story's narrator is self-sacrificing, self-righteous, defensive, afraid, inflected with that protective love for family that tips over into anger, laying himself bare before us. The climactic scene in the club when the narrator finally goes to hear Sonny play might be—and I don't think I'm overstating this—otherwise known as the best description of music ever written.

But I want to talk about all those windows, the way they hold and shape this wealth of material, the way they frame mystery. To begin with, landscape in fiction, particularly in a first-person narration like "Sonny's Blues," is always a projection of character. Each time the narrator looks out the window, Baldwin is gesturing to the larger world that includes, and lies beyond, the narrator, and that illuminates the deep-space mystery of interiority. These are pivot points in the story, cueing us to crucial instances of character development, shifts that prefigure revelation.

In the very first paragraph of the story, the narrator considers "the darkness which roared outside" the subway window as he reads about his brother's arrest for heroin possession in the newspaper on his way to work. We are immersed with him in the aural experience—the roar of the train itself as it hurtles through a tunnel. We feel the darkness expand well beyond that which exists on the literal level of the story to include the endemic, intergenerational racism particular to the United States, which is not discussed in the article about Sonny's arrest but should be.

Then, in the first scene, the narrator is getting ready to leave his classroom at the end of the school day, the news of Sonny's recent arrest for drug possession very much on his mind. Baldwin doesn't have his narrator look inside; there would be nothing there for the reader to see. I once visited a friend in a psychiatric hospital. She was in the throes of a psychotic break and delusional, but she was, as people so often are when they're in the throes of a psychotic break and delusional, making a lot of sense. At one point, she said, "They keep telling me to look inside of myself." She looked down at her stomach and shrugged. "But I don't see anything." That, to me, is the very definition of the quagmire of first-person interiority. There's nothing to see. When in doubt, look out the window. There's always something to see.

By looking out, Baldwin brings us in. At first, the noise from the school courtyard comes in through the window. The narrator "listened to the boys outside, downstairs, shouting and cursing and laughing. Their laughter struck me for perhaps the first time. It was not the joyous laughter which—God knows why—one associates with children. It was mocking and insular, its intent to denigrate. It was disenchanted, and in this, also, lay the authority of their curses." Then Baldwin turns his narrator's gaze, and ours, out the window to the courtyard: "I stood up and walked over to the window and looked down into the courtyard. It was the beginning of the spring and the sap was rising in the boys. A teacher passed through them every now and again, quickly, as though he or she couldn't wait to get out of that courtyard, to get those boys out of their sight and off their minds." We have yet to meet Sonny, but in the scattering schoolboys and their teachers, we begin, on a subterranean level, to grasp the complexity of the narrator's relationship with his brother (he'd prefer not to look and not to see). There's also the gesture to the larger world of the story and the world beyond the story, a world in which young black boys are at risk of not being seen, and much, much worse. But even as Baldwin is showing us the narrator's (and by implication the world's) desire to avert his gaze, he trains the reader's gaze on those same boys. He cultivates curiosity about their lives as they disappear beyond the frame of the window. The gesture to what's offstage is similar to the way the secret lives of characters suggest one piece torn from a whole cloth. Who are these boys? What is the rest of their lives?

The next window isn't a proper window. It's a door, but it's still a frame that contains and allows us to see something a little messier. It appears just after the narrator's conversation with a friend of Sonny's who has confirmed that Sonny has gone to jail for heroin possession, as the narrator begins to "listen more carefully." The doorway, another frame, cues us—check out *this* view—to another incremental evolution of the narrator:

> We were in front of a bar and he [Sonny's friend] ducked slightly, peering in, but whoever he was looking for didn't seem to be there. The juke box was blasting away with something black and bouncy and I half watched the barmaid as she danced her way from the juke box to her place behind the bar. And I watched her face as she laughingly responded to something someone said to her, still keeping time to the music.

Wyeth's first window painting, *Wind from the Sea*, began when he went to the attic bedroom of the Maine home of his friend Christina Olson (the subject of *Christina's World*). He'd gone up there to make a study of a dormer window, and something unexpected happened—when he opened a different window to let in some air, an ocean breeze fluttered the dusty, translucent curtains, and the birds crocheted on the lace looked to be flying. He painted what he saw over a portrait he'd been making of Christina. The window framed the more ethereal eeriness of the lace birds fluttering to life, and that spooky curtain became the scrim through which we see the view out the window—a dirt road leading to a sliver of ocean and on the horizon a forest in shadows and the Olson family graveyard. Wyeth said of the window painting that it was a portrait of Christina, who suffered from a debilitating neurological disease and could no longer walk up the stairs to the room where the lace birds flew, and, indeed, she's been absorbed into the painting, into that view of the road disappearing into the distance. The wind through the window was a spooky chance occurrence, and Wyeth wanted to translate that feeling of accident and surprise, that feeling of wonder.

It's difficult to capture a sense of accident and surprise in fiction, but something similar happens when Baldwin's narrator glimpses the dancing barmaid only half visible behind the bar, responding to something he can't hear from someone whom the narrator can't see at all. The glimpse feels random, and there are things the narrator can't grasp here, in the same way there are things about Sonny that he can't grasp. These qualities may elude him, and us, but still, Baldwin suggests, it is worth paying attention to those things that dance by, seen out of the corner of the eye. To be returned to uncertainty, unfathomability, unknowing, especially in those moments we think we know it all. In that barmaid we notice the combination of coincidence and chance. She happened to dance by in the same instant the narrator looked into the bar. What he sees feels as improvised as one of Sonny's jazz solos, digressive but relevant. Related to this idea is the fleeting insight the narrator offers us into the sudden death of his two-year-old daughter, a fact so painful it is buried in the middle of the story; buried, but crucial to the narrator learning to hear his brother. "My trouble," the narrator tells us, "made his real."

The window with the most expansive view is situated in the key scene of the story. In an effort to help him understand how critical it is for him to be there for Sonny, the narrator's mother tells him the story of the death of his uncle who was killed by a group of white men who ran him over with a car and left him to die in front of the narrator's father.

Moments before his mother tells the story, the narrator has a memory that includes a window. He begins the memory as an adult, but soon it includes all of the many times he sat by this window in his parents' living room:

> She'd be sitting on the sofa. And my father would be sitting in the easy chair, not far from her. And the living room would be full of church folks and relatives. There

they sit, in the chairs all around the living room, and
the night is creeping up outside, but nobody knows
it yet. You can see the darkness growing against the
windowpanes and you hear the street noises every
now and again, or maybe the jangling beat of a
tambourine from one of the churches close by, but
it's real quiet in the room. For a moment nobody's
talking, but every face looks darkening, like the sky
outside. And my mother rocks a little from the waist,
and my father's eyes are closed. Everyone is looking
at something a child can't see.

He is many ages at once here, inhabiting the child's
view and the adult's view simultaneously, creating a
double-barreled effect. Baldwin is alluding to big, abstract ideas: the moment adulthood begins to seep
into a child's consciousness; the end of innocence; the
cyclical, generational nature of racism and the fight
to endure. One feels the story growing, like the darkness outside the window, which echoes the "darkness
which roared outside" the subway window when the
narrator read about Sonny's arrest. The growing darkness outside the window and the narrator's growing
awareness of the dangers of the world are inextricable.
In order for the reader to understand the metaphorical
darkness, the reader must experience the literal darkness out the window. The unparaphrasable content of

fiction, its mystery, exists because it is, first and foremost, a visceral experience. It is Nabokov's tingle in the spine. Fiction begins, always, in the body.

Near the end of the story, the narrator wanders the house, debating whether to search Sonny's room for drugs. He's at a loss. And what does Baldwin do? He is still and he has his narrator be still. Baldwin, so that we may see the narrator's jagged restlessness, is patient and attentive. He has his narrator look out the window onto Seventh Avenue and see something he's seen before—an old-fashioned revival meeting—as if he is seeing it for the first time: "Not a soul under the sound of their voices was hearing this song for the first time, not one of them had been rescued. Nor had they seen much in the way of rescue work being done around them." Baldwin is preparing us for the scene in the club, preparing us to really listen to Sonny, to really see him. The narrator doesn't make the connection with Sonny overtly. He doesn't need to. The narrator looks long and hard out this window. Baldwin lingers on this scene for an entire page, describing the "cuckoo's nest" hair of the woman watching the woman with the tambourine; the "conked hair reddish and metallic in the pale sun" of the barbecue cook; and a man who "fumbled in his pockets for change and stood holding it in his hand impatiently." This impatient, fumbling man turns out to be Sonny. The narrator hasn't recognized him, not at first. When Sonny walks away, the narrator realizes he's never really noticed the way Sonny walks before. He's never paid close enough attention. It takes every word of those long three paragraphs to arrive at that moment. It's narrative stillness—patient, attentive, waiting. Looking out.

Haunted, searching, transcendent, these windows Baldwin has built into the house of his story admit both interior and exterior space in the view out or back in. Nancy K. Anderson, in a wonderful essay in the catalog for the Wyeth exhibit, writes that windows, historically the symbol of the eye, create a sense that "looking out triggered looking in." Baldwin's windows, too, focus the eye, training the gaze on the actual, concrete stuff of the world, which suggests the ethereal invisible swirl of the narrator's emotion.

Read "Sonny's Blues" again and you'll start to notice other windows—when the narrator and Sonny are re- united upon Sonny's return from prison, they stare out separate cab windows at separate views of the same Harlem at "houses exactly like the houses of our past"; the narrator's mother "kept looking out into the streets" as she tells the narrator the story of his uncle for the first time; Sonny moves out of the narrator's view of the revival meeting in the street, coming in- side to stand beside him to look out the same window onto the same view only, of course, without Sonny in it. These smaller windows remind you that the narrator is telling *his* story, not his mother's, not Sonny's, whose perspectives are different and unknowable. What is unknowable is part of what the story is about. The narrator is giving us his view. You'll notice that Sonny walks away from a window—away from that view of the narrator's—as he tries to explain to the narrator what it feels like to be Sonny, something the narrator can't see. It's only when he's done trying that Sonny turns back to the window, at which point he cuts to the heart of the matter, saying plainly something that is apparent to both men: "You're my brother."

After all of that looking out and looking in, Baldwin has readied us for the scene in the club when the narrator is, finally, able to truly listen to Sonny. "Sonny's Blues" moves in the opposite direction to another famously sonic story, James Joyce's "The Dead"; where "The Dead" moves from a clattery party and arrives in the snowy silence of a hotel room where Gabriel watches Greta sleep, "Sonny's Blues" moves from the isolation of the subway car to Sonny's "kingdom," a nightclub full of people and music. And not just any music— the final song Creole the bandleader kicks into is *Am I Blue*. Sonny, we are told, is a Charlie Parker fan and, in the bebop tradition, the band—and Sonny—have taken a jazz standard and made it their own. After all the literal windows in the story, the final scene serves as a metaphoric window onto Sonny for the narrator, and a window onto the narrator for us. In Sonny's solo, when he makes *Am I Blue* his own, the narrator both hears the inimitability that is Sonny and experiences a synesthetic, intergenerational epiphany: "I saw my mother's face again, and felt, for the first time, how the stones of the road she had walked on must have bruised her feet. I saw the moonlit road where my father's brother died." It all comes together in an instant, leaving as it arrives, as instances do, one in the grander scheme of a million instances. The world, the darkness roaring outside, still exists, "stretched above us, longer than the sky."

Mark Rothko once said Wyeth's paintings were "about the pursuit of strangeness." The windows in the paintings gathered together for the *Looking Out, Looking In* exhibit provide a view onto strangeness, those extraordinary and powerful forces—death, chance, love—that you can't see but are just around the corner. In "Sonny's Blues," Baldwin uses windows to frame his own variety of strangeness, providing the reader a view at once panoramic and exquisitely intimate, a view like no other.

Hauntings

I'm sometimes wary of the part of myself that is defiantly antifactual, jonesing for the next hit of mystery, willing to do anything to get it. This version of myself resembles the master miniaturist in Steven Millhauser's story "In the Reign of Harad IV." Millhauser's master miniaturist begins to make replicas of his miniatures, but smaller, miniatures of miniatures, initiating a process of copying and shrinking and copying and shrinking until the actual thing disappears. He has spent his days tending to the upkeep of King Harad IV's splendiferous toy palace with its six hundred teeny rooms, dungeon, and gardens; itty-bitty copper keys for the locks on the toy palace's itty-bitty dresser drawers; and a basket of apples, complete with a minute fly on the stem of one of the apples from the toy palace's orchard. But now he has grown restless—"as if he had come to a forbidden door at the end of a private corridor and heard, as he slowly turned the key, a sound of distant music"—and so he challenges himself to make a palace the size of a thimble, so small it requires a special magnifying glass to see it. And, slowly but surely, the master miniaturist reaches for a world beyond what we can see. In willful defiance he "proposed to himself a plunge beneath the surface of the visible, the creation of a detailed world wholly inaccessible to the naked eye." The master miniaturist's apprentices think he's gone around the bend and, in a way, he has. He has submitted himself to a solitude that requires a willingness to reside in bafflement, an insistence upon it. He no longer dwells in the world of agreed-upon facts. The bend around which he's gone is the bend of the actual into something quite powerful. If realness were measured on a Richter scale of experienced feeling, then the master miniaturist's imaginary realm might be the most real of all.

After all of my references to things spectral, a proper ghost story is in order. A ghost story contains both varieties of mystery—the answer-seeking of the genre and the question-seeking of the literary quality; it offers us a view onto another type of *un*, the uncanny. The translation of *unheimlich*, that wonderful German word that gives us *the uncanny*, captures that which is unfamiliar: literally the *un*home. This unhominess is the state of affairs for the unnamed governess in Henry James's novella *The Turn of the Screw*. She feels the presence of the uncanny as she tends her two young charges at the country estate of Bly, which is (possibly) haunted by recently dead servants who may have (possibly) done unseemly things to one another and to the children.

The question the story hinges on but never quite answers has been the subject of a debate since its publication in 1898: Is the governess who narrates this tale losing it or are the ghosts of the recently dead servants, Peter Quint and Miss Jessel, the real deal? The tightrope of psychological ambivalence James walks means he never tells us definitively, and that's where the mystery resides, in that space between yes and no. Other basic plot points go unanswered: Why was Miles, the boy child, expelled from school? What is the governess's story? We're told she is the youngest daughter of a poor country parson, and things aren't going so smoothly with the family she left behind (she is "in receipt in these days of disturbing letters from home"), but beyond that, we don't know much about her except for what she tells us about the situation at Bly. The main instruction to the governess before the children's bachelor uncle sends her off to Bly is not *Make sure they eat their vegetables* but rather *Don't bother me no matter what.* What's behind his negligence? We're never told. The omission is convenient for the sake of the plot. These unanswered questions also mean we slide more easily into that space between yes and no, the intriguing chasm of maybe.

The Turn of the Screw begins with a familiar gothic trope. Before we get to the actual story, there's a lot of hullabaloo around a found manuscript from which we are three times removed. James was interested in the tradition of ghost stories and supernatural tales, and the opening setup is a primer on the virtues of *it was a dark and stormy night* storytelling. The novella opens with a tale about the visitation of a ghost, a story that holds the guests at the country party "sufficiently breathless." As it should, is the original, pregoverness first-person narrator's—and James's—point. But not so fast. If a story about the visitation of a ghost upon one child leaves guests breathless, why not a story about more ghosts and more children? "It's beyond everything," says the man in possession of the story. "For sheer terror?" asks the narrator. No, the man says, making a key distinction. It's not that simple. "For dreadful—dreadfulness!" He goes on. "For general un-canny ugliness and horror and pain." "Well then," the narrator says, "just sit right down and begin." In order to tell the dreadful tale, the man has to send home for a manuscript under lock and key, given to him by his former governess, now dead twenty years. The conceit of the story we eventually read is that it's an exact copy made by the original first-person narrator after the man he met at the party who told it to him originally passed it on to him upon his death. Not so unusually contorted a premise for its time—still, this distance from the thing itself contributes to the more traditional elements of mystery. We travel all that way on dry land

only then to be immersed in the underwater claustro-
phobia of the governess's first-person account, never
to surface again. We drown in the governess's saga,
which ends abruptly when Miles drops dead of fright.
It's never precisely clear why the governess wrote this
all down, or what she makes of her tale, never mind
what the narrator who presents it all to us makes of it
himself.

Sheer terror forces our eyes wide open. It's the full
monty. *Dreadfulness* and *general uncanny ugliness* is
more of a negligée—sheer, lace, anticipatory desire. The
second type of story engages our imagination in the
way that only things we almost see can. Is it there or
isn't it? In a grouchy review of *The Innocents*, the 1961
film version of *The Turn of the Screw* starring Deborah
Kerr, Bosley Crowther takes it to task for its "liminal
obscurity" and takes Kerr to task because she "neither
acts nor looks a repressed or inhibited woman. She
seems excessively normal and alive when she takes
the governess job." Ahem. It was 1961 and Crowther
hadn't seen what Truman Capote, who contributed to
the screenplay, saw in James's intentions—that *liminal
obscurity* was the point. Part of what makes James's
governess mysterious is precisely her normalness and
her aliveness when she takes that job. In the scene in
which Kerr, future governess, meets Michael Redgrave,
ironic, handsome bachelor uncle, Capote punches up a

crucial aspect of James's novel by having Redgrave ask Kerr, "Do you have an imagination?"

Imagination—its capacity for wonder—is at the heart of this tale. It's what allows the governess to do her job well. Of the beginning of her time with the children, she writes, "I walked in a world of their invention— they had no occasion whatever to draw upon mine; so that my time was taken only with being, for them, some remarkable person or thing that the game of the moment required." As her sense of isolation increases, as the housekeeper, Mrs. Grose, gradually divulges all she knows of the sordid history of the valet Peter Quint and the previous governess Miss Jessel, the greatness of the governess's imagination is what causes her to do the job poorly, reading the precocious, peculiar things the kids say as evidence of their being in cahoots with the ghosts of Peter Quint and Miss Jessel. That imagination is born, in part, from the depths of loneliness. That James was himself no stranger to loneliness makes the depths of the governess's loneliness, and the children's for that matter, even more heartbreaking.

Imagination and loneliness are powerful, dynamic forces, flowing one into the other and back again. The loneliness of the governess, instructed by the uncle to handle the strange land of the Bly estate on her own, is matched by the loneliness of these children, whose unspoken instruction from their uncle is: Raise yourselves. Is it any wonder Miles runs out into the dark of night as a way of flirting with his governess, and that Flora contents herself by playing with her creepy doll all by herself down by the scary lake? But we're trapped in the mind of an increasingly uneasy—to put it mildly—first-person narrator. Flame from the match of her loneliness to the wick of her imagination sets the story on fire. Just before the ghost of Peter Quint first appears to her from the top of one of the grand towers that flank the Bly house, she tells us, "One of the thoughts that, as I don't in the least shrink now from noting, used to be with me in these wanderings was that it would be as charming as a charming story suddenly to meet someone. Someone would appear there at the turn of a path and would stand before me and smile and approve."

The familiar tropes of the ghost story combine with the governess's yearning; together they create the perfect conditions. It's the perfect weather for ghosts. "Henry James's ghosts," Virginia Woolf wrote, "have nothing in common with the violent old ghosts—the blood-stained sea captains, the white horses, the headless ladies of dark lanes and windy commons. They have their origin within us. They are present whenever the significant overflows our powers of expressing it; whenever the ordinary appears ringed by the strange." I'd say James has it both ways with his ghosts in *The Turn of the Screw*.

Appearing at first in the twilight haze of dawn and dusk, all gloomy scowls and witchyness, they scare the bejesus out of you *and* they register as a wish fulfillment, the governess's longing made manifest. By the time the specter of Miss Jessel appears at the governess's schoolroom table, it's "clear noonday light" and she's using the governess's "pens, ink, and paper." She's a gratifying, shimmery double if ever there was one. Still, even as she is there, she is slipping away. No one else but the governess ever sees the ghosts, but for the story to achieve its effect, James makes sure readers feel as though they have too.

In the penultimate scene, a distressed Mrs. Grose shields an even more distressed Flora, carrying her off, away from the governess, who has just insisted the little girl confirm that Miss Jessel's spirit self is floating *right there*, across the lake from them. "No evening I had passed at Bly," the governess tells us, "had the portentous quality of this one; in spite of which—and in spite also of the deeper depths of consternation that had opened beneath my feet—there was literally, in the ebbing actual, an extraordinarily sweet sadness." I love that. The *ebbing actual*. An actual that isn't actual at all but porous and dissolving. There is no grabbing hold of it. We, along with James's lonely, imaginative narrator, are engaged in a combination of seeing and unseeing. The loneliness of imagination and the imagination of loneliness palpable—they are ghosts here too, part of the ebbing actual.

Jean Rhys's *Voyage in the Dark* shares with James a deep, abiding interest in hauntings and a belief in ghosts. *Voyage in the Dark* isn't a traditional ghost story, but like many of Rhys's novels, it is a novel of displacement and alienation at the heart of which is an anguished homesickness, which becomes a specter. The sensibility is that of Anna Morgan, the nineteen-year-old narrator from a small unnamed island in the West Indies (Rhys herself was from the island of Dominica) who finds herself in England working as a chorus girl. She lives, bewildered, in this strange in-between zone, betwixt and between.

Listen to Anna:

It was as if a curtain had fallen, hiding everything I
had ever known. It was almost like being born again.
The colours were different, the smells different, the
feeling things gave you right down inside yourself was
different. Not just the difference between heat, cold;
light, darkness; purple, grey. But a difference in the
way I was frightened and the way I was happy. I didn't
like England at first. I couldn't get used to the cold.
Sometimes I would shut my eyes and pretend that the
heat of the fire, or the bed-clothes drawn up round

me, was sun-heat. . . . It was funny, but that was what
I thought about more than anything else—the smell
of the streets and the smells of frangipanni and lime
juice and cinnamon and cloves, and sweets made of
ginger and syrup, and incense after funerals or Corpus
Christi processions, and the patients standing outside
the surgery next door, and the smell of the sea-breeze
and the different smell of the land-breeze.

Sometimes it was as if I were back there and as if
England were a dream. At other times England was the
real thing and out there was the dream, but I could
never fit them together.

The sensibility here is akin to an exposed nerve ending. This is where the novel begins—in this exposed
nerve, right there in that wound. The ghost of Anna's
home is here with her in England, and so, even as she's
in England, she is somewhere else too. She is there on
the page, but she is tugged by these ghostly memories,
hovering around the edges of the pages as well. *Voyage
in the Dark* takes place between the wars, and Anna,
living in England after the death of her parents, is a chorus girl at the end of a tour of provincial English towns.
Her life is haphazard, a succession of identical boarding
houses; of nasty landladies who raise disapproving eye-
brows; of roommates who, like Anna, are looking for
husbands to rescue them from their haphazard lives.

They find plenty of men, but these men are looking to be rescued in the other direction, from the marriages they're already in. While all of the chorus girls live on the fringe, Anna is doubly removed, alienated from this alienated world because she is not English; her fellow chorus girls, the closest thing she has to friends, call her "the Hottentot."

"I'm nineteen," says Anna at one point, "and I've got to go on living and living and living." As with an exposed nerve, the pain radiates outward from the central point, engulfing you until you can't pinpoint its origin. The sensibility is skinless, stripped bare; even so, Rhys immerses herself in a mind that is not extinguished under the weight of this life. Rather, it flickers on, illuminating her current circumstances (which include heartbreak by one man; an accidental pregnancy by another; and an abortion that nearly kills her), giving us intermittent glimpses of that past, those ghosts that suggest an entire history.

Often Rhys's characters are described as beyond wretched and autobiographical. Here's a quote from a Michiko Kakutani review of Carole Angier's biography of Rhys, describing these characters (and Rhys)—as "victims, frail, unhappy women, with similar stories: not enough love, not enough money, not enough hope or will. Expectations of romance and happiness inevitably give way to loss and humiliation; and life devolves into a succession of shabby hotel rooms and alcohol-fueled bouts of depression." To which I say: my kind of book. Still, it's important to understand that Rhys was a consummate craftswoman. So much so, by the way, that she held a grudge against her editor for years, accusing her of publishing her most famous novel, *Wide Sargasso Sea*, before it was finished. Why wasn't it finished? There were, Rhys believed, two unnecessary words still in the manuscript: *then* and *quite*.

My point is that the voice Rhys has built out of words for Anna is muscular, not frail. Here, for example, in the midst of receiving a lecture from her most recent roommate for staying out too late with another random guy, is Anna: "The long shadows of the trees, like skeletons, and others like spiders, and others like octopuses. 'I'm quite all right; I'm quite all right. Of course, everything will be all right. I've only got to pull myself together and make a plan.' . . . It was one of those days when you can see the ghosts of all the other lovely days. You drink a bit and watch the ghosts of all the lovely days that have ever been from behind a glass." And here she is, a few drinks in, having excused herself to go to the bathroom while on a date with Walter, the heartbreaker, seeing one of those ghosts from a lovely day:

> I looked out of the bedroom window and there was a
> thin mist coming up from the ground. It was very still.

Before I came to England I used to try to imagine a night that was quite still. I used to try to imagine it with the crac-cracs going. The verandah long and ghostly—the hammock and three chairs and a table with the telescope on it—and the crac-cracs going all the time. The moon and the darkness and the sound of the trees, and not far away the forest where nobody had ever been—virgin forest. We used to sit on the verandah with the night coming in, huge.

Anna may well be a victim of circumstance—without enough money or enough love or enough hope or enough will—but her narration is driven by diction and syntax that reflect the singular lyricism of her mind. Even when that mind is trapped in a shabby hotel room, even in the throes of an alcohol-fueled bout of depression, even when, in the midst of company, her only companions are ghosts, it is lyrical. The sensibility at work—part raw nerve and part medium—is so fine-tuned that it picks up the high frequency of ghosts only this nineteen-year-old chorus girl far from home can hear.

And those ghosts are everywhere in this novel, suggesting other ghosts, other lives. My favorite ghost reference—my favorite line in the novel—comes when, in the midst of pleading with Walter, Anna looks around a posh Marylebone hotel and thinks, "The people there were like upholstered ghosts." I'm not even sure what it means, but I say, right on. Anna is haunted by so many things—the people living lives beyond her reach, sipping champagne all around her as her own life goes off the rails—but Rhys makes clear, by weaving it deftly throughout the narrative, that Anna is haunted most by the life she left behind, so present it is as if it is still happening. Part of the mystery Rhys is preoccupied by is the mystery of memory itself, the miracle of the mind as it retrieves, conjures, and otherwise merges past and present.

These ghost memories are delivered in fragments, which give us Anna's faraway life in the West Indies. The large, beautiful vase of the past has been broken and the million tiny shards have lodged in Anna's mind— the texture of the "black ribbed-wool stockings" and "brown kid gloves straight from England, one size too small" she wore every Sunday to church; the mango trees; a sky "hard, blue and close to the earth"; the creaking hammock ropes and the outer shutters "banging, like guns." The colors of home—"red, purple, blue, gold, all shades of green"—fill her senses as she lives amidst the less vibrant colors of England. People from her past parade without context through her thoughts, including a random woman with yaws who she tells us spoke to her, though we never learn what was said. "I thought I had forgotten about her," says Anna. "And now—there she is." There she is, and the past is here, alive, suggesting a life long gone, suggesting Anna before the novel begins, before the reader ever met her.

Often, there is no transition at all between the past and the present. Many of the memories begin with ellipses; it's in these that Anna resides. Chapter eight begins with an ellipsis—". . . I was walking along the passage to the long upper verandah which ran the length of the house in town"—and ends with the discovery of Uncle Bo with "long yellow tusks like fangs [that] came out of his mouth and protruded down to his chin—you don't scream when you are frightened because you can't and you don't move either because you can't . . . I had never seen false teeth before." Immediately following this memory, she tells us, "I read it again." Read what again? We don't know what she's read in the first place; we're still reeling, she's still reeling, from the memory of the false teeth. The *it* turns out to be a letter from a creepy friend of Walter's, asking her to return all of the letters she and Walter exchanged. Anna wonders at the association her mind has made between this letter and her uncle's false teeth, and then Rhys allows Anna to linger, no, to wallow, in the strange. The false teeth lead to a random jumble of associations from her past: "But I went on thinking about false teeth, and then about piano-keys and about that time the blind man from Martinique came to tune the piano and then he played and we listened to him sitting in the dark with the jalousies shut because it was pouring with rain and my father said, 'You are a real musician.'" The jumble ends with a man named Mr. Crowe, whom we've not met before, saying, "'You don't mean to say you're backing up that damned French monkey?' meaning the Governor, 'I've met some Englishmen,' he said, 'who were monkeys too.'" And there's the connection: Walter is a monkey, too. But every bit of that rambling series of images contributes to our larger sense of Anna. The soul may vanish when you look at it directly, but look at it sideways and it grows immense. The ghostly, fragmented memories of the past aren't past at all; they exist still within Anna.

As with Alice from Comyns's *The Vet's Daughter*, Anna has her own moment of levitation. It's not incidental that Comyns and Rhys were women writers during the interwar period and just after, when a lot was permitted and a lot was denied for women. No way forward? No way back? Levitate. After the nearly botched abortion, Anna is in and out of consciousness—once again, somewhere betwixt and between. Here's Anna: "I drank the gin and listened to them whispering for a long while. Then I shut my eyes and the bed mounted into the air with me. It mounted very high and stayed there suspended." She floats up and up. Away from the chatter in the room—her friend has finally called a doctor, who, upon learning she's taken quinine, laughs and says, "You girls are too naïve to live, aren't you?" Anna is still floating up and away, away from this body, this life, into the in-between place. She has become a spirit girl, and she will haunt you. You feel the movement of that spirit across the body of the novel. It is a force, that movement, big and mysterious and infinite.

Living in the Land of Un

Years after that impromptu camping trip in the pine forest, I asked my mother, Jane Barnes, who is also a writer, about her writing life. "Inchoate reaching in heartfelt darkness" was how she described it. Which, as it turns out, is a good way to describe the wonder I felt in the woods that night, the wonder I returned to when I was hypnotized. Over the years, I've heard echoes of my mother's phrase in various moods, in the faces of friends and lovers, in familiar and unfamiliar landscapes.

I like to imagine it might describe Isaac Babel's experience as he worried over the sentences that comprised his fictional surrogate, struggling to be a writer who would someday worry over his own sentences. Or Dezső Kosztolányi's as he revised and then revised again the scene in which Skylark contemplates her *I*-dom. Or Barbara Comyns's as she stumbled her way to the realization that Alice should levitate. Or Eudora Welty's when, the day after Medgar Evers's murder, she strived to get down on paper the murderous voice of Beckwith, as she wrestled with where that voice was coming from. Or Shirley Jackson's as the heat of Merricat welled up in her, and Jackson wrote as fast as she could to get that first searing paragraph onto the page before it burned itself up altogether. Or James Baldwin's as, after trying other things, he arrived at the structure that would allow "Sonny's Blues" to travel the years it took for his narrator to arrive at the fleeting connection with Sonny. Or W. G. Sebald's as, on his own wander, he composed his narrator's. Or Jean Rhys's as she arranged and rearranged the fragments of Anna's past. I won't ever know. But I do know I find myself inchoately reaching in heartfelt darkness when I sit down to write. It's how I felt when I sat down at my desk and struggled to translate the wonder of an impromptu camping trip in a Rhode Island pine forest, and the feeling I had under hypnosis of both performing and dissolving into the experience of my character, a nineteenth-century French man, lost in the world and lost to himself, who received therapeutic hypnosis from a psychiatrist in a Bordeaux asylum. It's how I felt as I stumbled my way into writing something new. I suspect—I hope—it's how I'll feel when I sit down to write years from now.

Inchoately reaching in heartfelt darkness has to do with searching, not finding. It has to do with that land of Un—uncertainty, unfathomability, unknowing—which, turns out, is where writers live most of the time. There are the howling wolves and, worse still, the howling writer, feeling her way intuitively in the dark. All that inchoate reaching, all that heartfelt darkness, it can be terrifying, that land of Un. How I dwell in that land has as much to do with why I'm there in the first place as it does with my methods for staying (self-hypnosis when a professional hypnotist isn't available, and a carrot-and-stick system wherein the carrot is dark chocolate and the stick is the void). The alternative is to close all the windows and to shut all the doors. I'd rather risk being afraid in order to feel more in relation to the world. What rewards there are for opening a window or two, and maybe even a door! For all the very same reasons that it's terrifying, Un is a bounteous land. There aren't many answers, but there are plenty of compelling questions, many of which will lead you on wild goose chases (otherwise known as stories and novels) and sometimes you will catch a glimpse of a wild goose.

I have at home a book of photography called *Moments of Writing: Camera Obscura*, by the Flemish photographer Alexandra Cool, which I find myself turning to a lot these days as I think about mystery in relation to my own work, in relation to writing as a vocation, and in relation to that aesthetic argument that art can and should undo us. In the introduction, Cool writes that she "wanted especially to photograph the work of writing itself." That is, amazingly, what she has done. She built a pinhole camera with a hole so tiny that the exposure time was half an hour; then she placed that camera on the desks of some hundred writers and asked them to act natural, to do what they would normally do when they sit down to write. Half an hour later, she retrieved the camera. The resulting photographs are a spirit portraiture of these writers. The writers appear shadowy, in motion. The more a writer moved, the blurrier she became. Some of the writers are spooky smudges. Cool has found a way to capture the wildness of the imagination. There it is, embodied, and yet it remains alluringly mysterious.

In *The Varieties of Religious Experience*, William James wrote, "We are alive or dead to the eternal inner message of the arts according as we have kept or lost this mystical susceptibility." It might be said of writing and reading that they are a variety of religious experience. Certainly they are a way of moving through, and being in relation to, the world. Mystery is the key ingredient. It allows us to experience the intangible and is a means of bridging the finite and the infinite. There's an aspect of infinity to mystery—an eternal becoming. That mystical susceptibility James speaks of—that willingness to reside in, and to make room for, mystery—is at the heart of making art.

Works Discussed

Abani, Chris. *Song for Night.*

Babel, Isaac. "Awakening."

Baldwin, James. "Sonny's Blues."

Bechdel, Alison. *Fun Home: A Family Tragicomic.*

Bowles, Jane. "Camp Cataract."

Coetzee, J. M. *Waiting for the Barbarians.*

Comyns, Barbara. *The Vet's Daughter.*

Hempel, Amy. "What Were the White Things?"

Jackson, Shirley. *We Have Always Lived in the Castle.*

James, Henry. *The Turn of the Screw.*

James, William. *The Varieties of Religious Experience.*

Kosztolányi, Dezső. *Skylark.*

Millhauser, Steven. "In the Reign of Harad IV."

O'Connor, Flannery. "Good Country People."

Rhys, Jean. *Voyage in the Dark.*

Sebald, W. G. *The Rings of Saturn.*

Welty, Eudora. "Where Is the Voice Coming From?"

Yoon, Paul. *Snow Hunters.*

Acknowledgments

I discovered the story of the spirit photographer Édouard Buguet in Martyn Jolly's mesmerizing *Faces of the Living Dead: The Belief in Spirit Photography* (Mark Batty Publisher). Some of the material in this book appeared in slightly different form as essays in *A Public Space, New England Review, New Ohio Review,* the *American Scholar,* and the *New York Times Book Review,* and in the anthology *A Kite in the Wind* (Trinity University Press); and as lectures at the Bread Loaf Writers' Conference and the MFA Program for Writers at Warren Wilson College. I'm grateful to the editors at those publications and to my colleagues and students at Bread Loaf, the University of Maryland, and Warren Wilson. Thank you to Steve Woodward for his incisive editing, and Fiona McCrae, Jeffrey Shotts, and everyone at Graywolf; to Charles Baxter for his inimitable insight and guidance; to the BAU Institute and the Bogliasco Foundation for fellowships that provided mysterious views out to sea. And to Michael Parker for the Natural Bridge, with its own mysterious view out to sea.

Permission Acknowledgments

Page 14: Photograph by Édouard Buguet © College of Psychic Studies London, 2016.

Page 31: *Mons. Leymarie and Mons. C. with Spirit of Edouard Poiret* by Édouard Buguet. Wm. B. Becker Collection/PhotographyMuseum.com. Copyright © MMXVI The American Photography Museum, Inc.

Page 34: *Self-Portrait* by Vivian Maier. © Estate of Vivian Maier/Maloof Collection. Courtesy Howard Greenberg Gallery, New York.

Page 80: From *Fun Home: A Family Tragicomic* by Alison Bechdel. Copyright © 2006 by Alison Bechdel. Reprinted by permission of Houghton Mifflin Harcourt Publishing Company. All rights reserved.

Page 136: *Rui Coias - werkend aan* A Ordem do Mundo (1/3/2007) © Alexandra Cool. From *Moments of Writing: Camera Obscura* (Lannoo, 2010).

MAUD CASEY is the author of three novels, most recently *The Man Who Walked Away*, and a short story collection, *Drastic*. Her essays and book reviews have appeared in the *New York Times Book Review*, *Washington Post Book World*, *Salon*, *A Public Space*, and *Literary Imagination*. She is the grateful recipient of the Italo Calvino Prize, the St. Francis College Literary Prize, and a Guggenheim Fellowship. She lives in Washington, DC, and teaches at the University of Maryland.

The text of *The Art of Mystery* is set in Warnock Pro, a typeface designed by Robert Slimbach for Adobe Systems in 2000. Book design by Wendy Holdman. Composition by Bookmobile Design & Digital Publisher Services, Minneapolis, Minnesota. Manufactured by Friesens on acid-free, 100 percent postconsumer wastepaper.